LITTLE

ALTERNATE UNIVERSE

by

Helen Wernlund

Copyright 2016 by Helen Wernlund
ISBN-13:978-1514265673

ISBN-10:1514265672

Table of Contents

Foreword   7

Life Changes   9

Where Did the Socks Go?   11

My First Car   15

Moving In   19

Catalogs   23

Food   27

Clotheslines   31

The Canoe Trip   37

Finding Martin Luther   41

Crossword Puzzles   45

Unhinged By Technology   49

Words to Live By?   53

Confirmation Class   57

Getting From Here to There   61

You Can't Make This Stuff Up   65

Stress Relief   69

Dancing   73

Bathroom Tissue   77

Gardening   81

Pea Soup Is Forever   85

A Plethora of Pastors   89

Old and Healthy? Yes, Indeed   93

The Joy of Sox   97

Languages and Accents   101

Smoking   105

Oh, Those Clothes!   109

Who's Keeping Time   113

Coffee   119

Do You Speak English?   123

Out, Out, Foul Tonsils   127

Music   131

Don't Fall Down   137

Going to the Beach   143

JIFFLE   149

Happiness   157

Mental Meanderings   161

Working   165

Leaving Home   177

On Being a Snowbird   179

The Destruction of Teakettles   183

About Ed   187

Where Did the Socks Go This Time?   195

Gadgets   199

What Do You Do With a Boomba?   205

The Lure of Water   209

The Show Must Go On   215

Worst Winter Ever   223

Christmas Memories   225

Acknowledgments   227

About the Author   229

FOREWORD

You may have gathered from the title of this book that I'm a believer in the existence of an alternate universe. Too many things have disappeared, practically in front of my eyes, and then reappeared again later, for me to think otherwise. And it certainly explains some of the peculiar things that happen around here! Lucky for me, I have a whole community of friends and neighbors who are willing to indulge me in this, and who tell me they enjoy hearing about what happens in the alternate universe, as well as in the wanderings of an eighty-year-old mind.

I live in a retirement community in Eastern Pennsylvania now. Of course, Lutherburgh, as it appears in this book, is a fictional community which just happens to have a lot in common with the delightful place I call home. As its name indicates, our community has a relationship with the Lutheran Church, and that's one of the things that makes it a really good place to be.

We have our own literary publication, giving the residents a forum to say whatever they please about their lives, past and present, and to share their opinions and ideas. I've been fortunate to have many of my essays published in that periodical. Members of our writers' group have urged me to compile them into a book, and I thought, as I often do, "How hard could it be?"

Well, it's been a lot harder than I expected, but the process has provided great mental exercise, and I hope you will enjoy reading what it's like to live in retirement, as well as some musings on childhood, family life, and just having fun.

All of the stories included here are more or less true as I remember them. Some characters are composites of several people, and the names of some places and people have been changed to protect the innocent and to protect me from a lawsuit. So if you think you recognize yourself, you really don't, and I'll deny I ever knew you.

Happy reading!

Author, age 3

LIFE CHANGES

When I was 50, newly divorced, and trying to figure out what I would do with the rest of my life, my widowed pal, Linny, and I decided we would start a commune when we got old. Both of us had rather small houses at the time, but why let reality stand in the way of an especially good idea?

We worked out a plan exactly to our liking. Our fellow housemates would be carefully selected on the basis of relative good health and their ability to bring a skill or an interest to our little family, such as gourmet cooking, a love of housework, gardening, auto maintenance, and so on. But above all, they would have to be INTERESTING!

We understood that we would need a big house, with six or eight or even ten bedrooms, each with private bath, and perhaps a sitting area, too, so that people could hide out if too much community became a problem. We'd want a large kitchen and dining room, a den or finished basement for a game room and laundry, and a backyard with shade trees and benches.

If all went well, we thought a swimming pool would be a nice touch, along with a koi pond and meditation space. We thought that a ten-car garage would be ideal, but decent parking for ten, plus guests, would suffice. I should probably mention here that Linny was working as a teacher's aide, and I had been unhurriedly working on a bachelor's degree while doing part-time office work for a small law firm. Neither of us was enjoying a lavish lifestyle.

Well, time marched on, as it always does, and so did Linny and I. Her solution for her senior years was a trailer on a Florida canal and a manufactured home in Riverhead, N.Y. Mine became Lutherburgh. What do you know? I live in a very big house, with a whole apartment all my own, not just a bed, bath and sitting room!

My New Home

There are people who cook and do the housekeeping very well indeed, and cut the grass, and *everyone* is interesting. I do miss my old garage, but there's plenty of parking right outside my window. I can be sociable, or I can hide out, and it seems so far that no one is going to criticize me for the choices I make. I don't even feel that old anymore. I feel kind of …. golden. And I intend to keep it that way!

* * *

WHERE DID THE SOCKS GO?

While I was putting away the laundry the other day I noticed that I had a large number of single socks in the drawer. Since I like colorful socks it was easy to see that no two were alike. After rummaging around for a while I knew that "the worst" had happened. My socks had left for the alternate universe!

Don't laugh. You know that the alternate universe exists. In fact, I suspect that there may be more than one, since some things that go away come back, while others do not. One of our neighbors mentioned recently that he had put an important paper on his dining room table, gone out to lunch, and returned to find that the paper was nowhere to be found. I ask you, where else could it have gone, except into the alternate universe?

It was surely not stolen by gypsies while he was away. Gypsies are known for stealing small children, not paperwork, so while they might have found their way into his apartment, they certainly wouldn't have run off with his tax forms. On second thought, perhaps alternate universe gypsies may find tax forms appealing …. but who knows. While our neighbor eventually agreed with me, he wasn't comforted, since the time of return from the alternate universe is totally unpredictable, although in my experience the place of return is usually somewhere close to where the thing went missing.

My most dramatic experience of the alternate universe was when one half of my favorite pair of earrings disappeared. These beautiful amethyst and silver drops had spoken to me at a craft fair in Florida and I hadn't resisted their siren call. A year later, back in New York, I found a bracelet that matched them exactly. I was really excited about unexpectedly acquiring a set of beautiful jewelry, with my birthstone no less, and I wore them quite often.

One evening while preparing for bed I realized that I was wearing only one earring! I had been running around all day. Where could it have gone? After searching the carpets and corners of my rooms, I headed out to my car for a look around. No earring there, either. It was gone, and I was sure it was gone forever.

Time passed, actually several years passed, and I had pretty much forgotten about the earring although I wore the bracelet from time to time. Then one day, as I was taking some groceries from the back seat of my car, I saw a glint of silver under the corner of the floor mat in the back. I picked up the mat, and there was my long-lost earring! That car had been washed many times, the inside vacuumed, and people had come and gone, with and without their own bags and paraphernalia, and there was no earring. Now there was. So where else could it have been all that time, except in the alternate universe?

More recently, I managed to "lose" my favorite pill box, a small heart-shaped one with an enameled reproduction of two of Michelangelo's cherubs on top, given to me by my friend Chris on her return from a tour in Italy. It had been on the table in the dining room while I had dinner, and I am sure I put it in my pants pocket when I left, but the next morning I realized it was not in its usual place on the shelf next to my front door. I checked the pockets of pants and sweater …. no pill box. Yesterday, there it was, in my pants pocket. Of course, I do have two pairs of pants of the same color, so I suppose it *might* have been in the other pair, but I wore both of them more than once in the intervening time, so there's really nowhere else that pillbox could have been except in the alternate universe.

Many little items have disappeared over time, only to show up again when I had finally decided they were gone forever. Others, I fear, are scattered around the alternate universe like so much space debris in our own world.

The one thing I've been looking for since 1995 is the gold cross my parents gave me for my tenth birthday. It disappeared, and it hasn't returned. I missed it so much that I bought a look-alike; it just isn't the same. But I haven't lost faith in my theory of the alternate universe. I think I dropped the cross in the dressing room of a Macy's store on Long Island, and although I went back to inquire several times, no one turned it in.

When and if it finally came back I wasn't there, but someone else may have been so I must assume it's lost to me forever. If only it could have reentered this universe where its owner was, rather than from where it disappeared, I'm sure I would have gotten it back long ago.

* * *

MY FIRST CAR

Unlike most people I know, I didn't have a car of my own (that is, registered in my name; I had helped to pay for three of them) until I was 48 years old.

Growing up in Brooklyn, I had no need for a car. My father didn't own one until I was in high school. He proudly purchased a little blue Datsun and made my mother a nervous wreck, even though he was a good driver. Being a stubbornly independent Swede, he didn't have much use for "No Parking" signs, and whenever they went shopping mom was in a constant state of anxiety from the moment they headed out, sure that they would come home with a $2,000 parking ticket and a bad reputation when the neighbors found out.

"My" car became mine due to an unfortunate problem of my then husband's, when, in a state of abject contrition, he offered to give me a car of my own …. and he would pay for it himself. I knew it was a bribe but I was angry enough not to care. It was too good a deal to pass up, and I would think about the implications later.

We went to the dealership and there, on a platform in the middle of the showroom, was the cutest car I had ever seen! It was very small; I think it was a Chevy Cricket, but it was long ago and memory fails. The car was YELLOW and it had a hatchback and a roof rack. Wow! When I looked at that car I was 18 years old all over again.

My husband conferred with the salesman while I stood in ecstasy, admiring the sheer beauty of that vehicle. "Well," he said, "this is the only one I can afford. Too bad you won't want it. It has a stick shift." But it was too late! I was in love with that little yellow bug. "That's okay," I said. "I'll learn to drive it," adding to myself, as I often do, "How hard could it be?"

Little Yellow Car

Well, I guess we all know about Famous Last Words! My sons took me out in the car over one weekend and pronounced me fit to drive. Actually, it wasn't too hard. Long Island, where we lived then, was mostly flat, and while the kids obviously forgot that stick shifts and hills can be incompatible for a novice, I didn't even know there was anything to worry about … until my friend Linny's son got married.

I went alone to the wedding. It was lovely, though I wasn't looking forward to the reception with no dancing partner in tow. However, I couldn't disappoint Linny by staying home. So I headed out on the Long Island Expressway to the catering hall, complimenting myself for actually arriving at the site with no mishaps, and then turned in to the driveway. Oh, my! I had forgotten that The Empire sat in splendor at the top of a very steep hill!

By this time I had discovered that hills could be difficult, but I hadn't yet encountered such a steep one. I decided that I could make it if I waited until there were no cars in sight at the top of the hill and I could make a straight run for it, so I sat with a line of cars filled with eager wedding guests forming behind me, and when all seemed clear, I started up the hill.

Uh, oh! The car at the top stopped dead, and, consequently, so did I. What was I going to do now? I completely blanked out about stepping on brakes and gas together and using the hand brake …. wait, wait, where did the clutch go? …. and what am I supposed to do with it? (You can see that I have put the details of this experience mostly out of my mind, which I began to do from the day that I sold that car.)

I decided I could best solve the problem by letting my yellow buggy roll slowly back down the hill, so that I could get a roaring start again at the bottom and reach my destination, which was looking like the first hill of heaven by this time, in one quick swoop.

Unfortunately, there were a number of cars behind me. I started s l o w l y backward, which seemed to disconcert the person behind me. He, in turn, started backing up, and as I looked out my rearview mirror, it seemed to me that cars were flying backwards in all directions. That was probably just a symptom of my panic, because I managed to get down the hill and, finally, up again, without causing any crack-ups or even fender-benders. How that happened, I will never know; I only know that I was a grateful person entering the catering hall.

Fortunately, there was a parking valet waiting to relieve me of my burden. He must have witnessed the whole incident because he gave me a big grin and a thumbs up as he took my keys. I was shaking like a gospel singer's tambourine when I reached the bar. (Don't worry. I was completely sober when I drove home. Single people know to do their drinking "up front" so that it's all cleared out of the system by evening's end.)

Ultimately I sold that car, after wrecking two transmissions. But it took me through a divorce and a kind of emotional resurrection, so it served me well, and though I've had other cars since, it is still my favorite.

* * *

MOVING IN

In May of 2011 I carted all my worldly goods from Deer Park, New York to Lutherburgh. Actually, Dan the Moving Man did the carting. My contribution was some dollars and lots of nerves and trauma. The move itself was only a matter of 150 miles, plus or minus a few, but I might as well have been going to Alaska. What to take? What to give away? And who would want it anyway?

When I arrived, hot and sweaty from travel, I was warmly (no pun intended) greeted by the admissions director with a camera in her hand. "This is good," she said, or something to that effect. "You're just in time to have your picture taken for the new directory." Trying to fix myself up was useless. Anyone who wants to look in the directory will understand.

The moving man was an angel! "I'll take you to the grocery store and K-Mart to help you get settled," he said. Oh, joy! Coming from Long Island I had no idea where anything was located. Some months later I found my way to Walmart, Target, various churches and the Farmers' Market. Of course, I have given my GPS (affectionately named "Irene,") a nervous breakdown, but so far there have been no reprisals.

I had hoped to find something better to wear for dinner that first night, but it wasn't possible. The clothes were tossed in the one closet, still on hangers but squashed together. Boxes were piled up on the floor, bed, dining room table, two dressers and the coffee table, leaving very little room to move around.

At six p.m. on that memorable moving day I staggered down to the dining room, still in the original shirt and Capri pants I had worn all day. The dining room was noisy and cheerful, with people eating and talking at round tables, square tables, in groups of two, four and more. I was alone but not for long. Two charming women invited me to join them, and that was the start of a long chain of delightful dinners with interesting and intelligent people.

Of course, there were adjustments to be made. A few months after the move, I came to realize that the toilet was just too high for my medium-short self. What to do, I wondered? Is this a subject I wish to discuss with the maintenance people? I was brought up in a family so prudish that one strove never to say that word aloud. How nice to discover that changing out a "t- - - - t" is a very straightforward job and can be done with a minimum of disruption.

The weird part of the whole project was finding myself sitting on the new one in the middle of my living room, while the maintenance man held onto the tank so it wouldn't tip over. "Yes," I said, too embarrassed to turn around and meet his gaze. "This fits." I left for an hour and when I returned, everything was taken care of.

Now the only thing I have left to deal with is the occasional stink bug that finds its way in. That's a critter I never heard of before coming to Pennsylvania.

I think they're kind of cute, to be honest, but I know better than to squash one.

Someday I'm going to have to do it, though, to find out for myself just how bad the stink really is.

* * *

CATALOGS

A few weeks before Christmas I opened my mailbox and found eight catalogs …. only two of which came from companies where I had ever shopped. Then one of our neighbors came along, opened his mailbox, and counted fourteen catalogs. Fortunately, he is still in good health and had the strength to cart them away with him. My problem with catalogs is that I can't resist looking at them, and once I've opened them it's only a short time before I'm making little checkmarks near the items I think I might like to have. It's rare, however, that I actually buy anything.

Sometime around 1986 one of the bargain-price catalogs advertised a set of two dozen pairs of variously colored knee-high stockings that I looked at for three or four years in a row. I think the price was about $12, but those were the days when I was very short of discretionary income, and I just couldn't commit. Sometime into the fifth year of checking these off in the catalog I finally decided to spring for the big $12, only to find that the shipping cost had gone up by $2. However, once I made up my mind I could not be deterred. When the next catalog arrived from that company, the knee-highs weren't in it. My decision finally to make the purchase was meant to be. I am still wearing some of the more exotically colored ones, so it was a good buy after all.

Catalogs work better for me than the Shopping Network would. I've avoided looking at that because I'm afraid I might be prone to impulse buying. With a catalog I have infinite time to revisit the pages where tempting items lurk. Almost always, after I've looked a few dozen times I decide I don't need it, and where would I put it anyway? But with a charming TV host to remind me that I must make a decision immediately, before whatever-it-is is all gone, I expect I would be lost, and broke.

Somehow my name has made it into the big time, and occasionally I get a catalog from one of the pricier stores. In one of them I saw a pencil that cost $450. How, I wondered, could a piece of lead in a blanket cost that much? Well, this one was made of silver and California cedar, and it had a sharpener in the end. Now I understood! But I decided not to get one, not even as a Christmas present for my son who has everything.

Just when I thought I had seen it all, another catalog arrived. On the cover there was a peculiar item that looked something like an enormous egg with an off-center hole cut into the top. A row of blue lights ringed the inside and on the bottom was some kind of white padding. Well, there it was again, on page 67: The Tranquility Pod. It weighs 350 lbs. and costs, are you ready for this? …. $30,000.

I can tell you, if I had one of these you might never see me again (except, of course, for meals). That padding inside is a temperature-controlled *waterbed*. It has a four-speaker sound system. It *vibrates,* for goodness sakes, and has a biofeedback system to synchronize your heart rate with the little blue light bulbs I mentioned, which also create mood lighting for "calming the mind." I ask you, how can anyone possibly live without this?

Perhaps Lutherburgh management would spring for one on each floor and we would all be able to relax into nirvana. There would definitely be a full sign-up sheet for that! Personally, I think it would be dangerous to get that relaxed.

Which reminds me, have any of you seen the commercial where people are singing "I want it," "I need it," "I want it *now*," and on and on? The more I see it the more annoyed I get. No wonder people are overcome with greed. What if we all walked around singing "I want world peace and I want it NOW." Would anyone pay attention?

* * *

FOOD

From my earliest childhood I've had an intimate relationship with my food. Perhaps it began when Baby Me, the youngest of five cousins in my small extended family, was coddled by loving *Tantas* who would tickle my chubby feet and call them *bullar*, which means "bun" in Swedish, though I may have spelled it wrong. I've been told that, while just barely verbal, I would extend my equally chubby leg, point regally toward my foot, and say *bullar*! meaning "pay attention to me!"

My mother explained to me that, when she was one among ten hungry children of Swedish farmers, as winter drew to an end the kids would go out to scavenge for potatoes that they might have missed during the harvest the year before. When she immigrated to America she swore, like Scarlett O'Hara, that she would never be hungry again. And believe me, we never were.

The family gathered at major holidays to enjoy stupefying dinners. We children were soon jaded by the magnificent spread that almost caused the dinner table to buckle under the sheer weight of culinary delights. But the child who ate the most got the most praise from the grownups, and in a family where kids were pretty much left to themselves, praise was at a premium and much to be desired.

Food-wise, Christmas could be delightful in a Swedish-American household. I couldn't wait to help my mom bake the wonderful cookies and coffee cakes, especially the ones enhanced with cardamom. I got to break the pods open and pulverize the cardamom seeds with my Dad's hammer. It was hard work but the results were fabulous.

When I started fourth grade in a new school, I had a six city-block walk to go home for lunch. At noon on an average day I would walk into an apartment that was redolent with the aroma of meatloaf, or maybe pork chops or sausage, with a pot of mashed potatoes at the ready and some nice, buttery vegetables. In the evening, when my father got home from work, we would have the same thing all over again, folowed by coffee and homemade cake, or possibly chocolate chip cookies, served formally in the living room because that's what the coffee table was for, after all. I don't ever remember being made to sit for hours at the dinner table to finish yukky food because I liked almost everything. Except oysters.

As an only child in the days before babysitters were widely employed I was taken everywhere by my parents. I wasn't spoiled, but I was used to throwing my two cents into any discussion that interested me. I think, in retrospect, that their childless friends had about all they could take from a talkative 11-year-old, when they gave me my first (and to this day, only) raw oyster at a barbeque on the beach. It was a BIG oyster, and once it was in my mouth I had no idea what to do with it. I had been raised to be polite, and spitting it out was not an option. Neither was choking in public. I remember prancing wildly down to the water's edge, splashing into the bay, and disgorging it, hopefully unseen, into the water. Suffering the indignity of being scolded for getting my clothes wet seemed preferable to being yelled at for being impolite or, worse yet, getting sick amidst the hot dogs and potato salad.

My mother was a great, but simple cook, and when I met my husband's family I was introduced to the pleasures of rare roast beef, salmon, and things made with shrimp. Where had this deliciousness been all my life? In the weeks before my marriage, when I expected the long-awaited intimate mother-daughter conversation (which never did take place) mom took me down to the Avenue to introduce me to her butcher. It was pretty clear what was important in our house!

I almost gave up my interest in food when my son, Steve, about age seven at the time, allowed his new retainer to get away from him in the grade school lunchroom. When he realized that it wasn't in his mouth, it was just too late! He came home crying; he knew the retainer was expensive and that his parents were not likely to be happy with the news. When I called the school to ask what, if anything, I could do to get it back, I was invited to come on down to the dumpster and see what I could find.

Resigned to what might lie ahead, I dragged on my high boots and headed back to school, Steve, also in boots, in tow. One look at that dumpster, filled with overcooked spaghetti and red sauce, almost did me in. I just couldn't climb in there, and I couldn't throw Steve in there, either. We went home and called the orthodontist.

People have a lot of different ways of approaching their food, and many Lutherburghers seem to really enjoy dessert, even if it's not necessarily good for them.

At dinner the other night, while some of us were contemplating the wisdom of finishing the large sundaes we had ordered, my friend Elizabeth made an astute observation that clinched the deal. "Remember the Titanic," she said, and we all happily dug in.

* * *

CLOTHESLINES

I grew up in a four-room apartment in a six-family walk-up in the middle of a block in the Bay Ridge neighborhood of Brooklyn. We lived on the top floor in the back, and our kitchen window opened onto a small courtyard where clotheslines were strung from our building to the one next door.

Since we were closest to the sunshine, our laundry always dried quickly, and when I was old enough to be trusted not to fall out the window, I was allowed to pull in the clean, fresh-smelling clothes. Perhaps that happy memory is what sparked my lifelong love of clotheslines.

As a young bride I took our clothes to the laundromat. We lived on the fourth floor of a four-story walk-up near Coney Island, and when our first child was born and I stopped working, my motherly instincts took over and I knew in my heart that I was duty-bound to wash the little bitty baby things by hand.

Since there was no one living overhead, I decided to dry the baby clothes on a line my husband installed on the roof, or "tar beach" as roofs were know in our circle. Bad move. The "Super" (superintendent of the building) stomped through the halls demanding to know who was desecrating his roof.

I begged, I pleaded, I snarled, I smiled, I even thought about curtseying, but finally agreed to take down the line. And that started a war of the wills. When a few days had passed, I'd sneak up to the roof and reinstall the clothesline. Some days later I would find it outside the apartment door. This silliness continued until we moved to "the country" (Long Island) where I ecstatically watched as my husband put up my very own clothesline in my very own backyard.

Clothesline at Deer Park

The wonderfulness of this experience dissipated rather quickly. When we bought our little house we knew that we were only two short blocks from the Long Island Railroad tracks and the junkyards that lined either side, but the realtor had assured us that, since a whole development of 500 homes was going up, the town was ready to shut down the yards. "Of course," he said, "our responsive town government is not going to allow a builder to erect a new community on a site that isn't perfectly located!" Were we stupid, or what? Just too young to know what we were doing, I guess, because we believed this reasonable logic. So I had to time my washing to days when the yards weren't burning junked automobiles, because the ashes would float in like grimy snowflakes, and everything on the clothesline would have to be re-washed.

Not too much later the town came through, and although the yards didn't have to close, their operations were strictly regulated, and my wash once again passed the bright and white test.

Even when we finally installed a dryer in the basement, the clothes went to the line whenever the weather cooperated. At the time, we had a front-loading washing machine and we could never seem to get it balanced properly, so during the spin cycle I would have to sit on it to keep it from walking across the basement floor. The neighbors would come over just to stand there and laugh.

Years later, when I moved to Ed's house, there were three long clotheslines running between four huge oak trees in the backyard. That was the longest clothesline I had ever seen, and I was delighted! (Clearly, it doesn't take much to make me happy.)

My spirits were dampened when I realized that I would have to walk through wet grass almost every time I wanted to hang the wash, since the South Shore of Long Island is usually very moist in the morning.

Clothesline at Ed's House

Ed was sympathetic. He managed to string a line from the back door to the side of the big shed in the backyard. However, while setting the screws into the shed, he messed up the mechanism for the automatic door. It was a costly clothesline …. but much easier to get to.

More years passed, and I moved to the little house owned by and next door to my church. "Oh boy!" I thought. I can have a clothesline here, too. But before the property committee could get around to putting one up, I realized it made no sense. Windowsills in both the back and front of the house got dirty quickly due to the traffic: cars, trucks and motorcycles constantly traversing the road right outside my door, on their way to an even bigger avenue 500 yards to the west.

I was thinking about trying it anyway, when I realized that the Luther League teens often used the yard between the church and my home for ball games and general hanging out. I could just imagine the giggles and snickers if they were to catch a glimpse of my utilitarian cotton dainties hanging on the clothesline!

So now I'm at Lutherburgh with a really nice washer-dryer combination, but I still miss my clothesline. Maybe I can string a line up across the balcony………?

Speaking of clotheslines on balconies, there was some discussion in the community awhile back about people hanging bathing suits on the balcony railings. I never saw this myself, but someone must have spoken to someone, because the topic was closed rather quickly and there were no more complaints.

But this gave some of us an idea which I would still like to implement one day, if I could only figure out how to do it.

Wouldn't it be fun, I thought, if the adventurous among us would hang clotheslines on our balconies for April Fools' Day? How long, I wondered, would it be before residents would start noticing?

To make this project instantaneously visible, I thought it would be even more fun if we could find a way to string clotheslines between the buildings. I have no instinct for distances so it's impossible for me to figure out how many feet of clothesline we would need; I think it would be *a lot!* But I'm pretty sure that some folks in each building would be into playing a big April Fools' prank like this.

Of course, we would have to do the installation in the dead of night, which would mean making the security guard complicit. And then we would have to find a ladder, and someone to climb it. I would be happy to involve my son, the carpenter, in this project, but somehow I think that even if he wanted to, his wife wouldn't let him.

April Fool!

So, fellow Lutherburghers, don't expect to find this happening in the near future, if at all. Not every great idea can be brought to fruition.

* * *

THE CANOE TRIP

Fifty years old and newly divorced, I realized that the pendulum in my cranial clock was swinging wildly between two zones: one, a sense of fear, even terror, about what lay ahead and, two, excitement and enthusiasm about exploring new ideas and adventures.

"Why not a canoe trip," I thought, when our Pastor decided he had room on the bus for some adults as well as the teens he would be chaperoning. After all, how hard could it be?

When the day arrived we headed for Dingman's Ferry, where we would climb into our canoes and paddle happily downstream to a campsite far, far away where dinner and tents for our overnight stay would be waiting for us.

Linny and I were the last to take off. We were among several couples and two other single women trailing the young people as dark clouds gathered overhead.

Everything seemed to be going well at first, as we paddled in to shore at a Ranger's station looking for a bathroom. There was none, but there was a large yellow and black sign that warned, "Rapids Ahead!"

Onto the River!

This was not good news!

Neither Linny nor I had canoed before and we were improvising as we went along. "What should we do?" we asked the Ranger. "Oh, just stay close to shore. You can get out and portage if you'd rather not shoot the rapids." Shoot the rapids? Was he insane? As we moved closer to the fatal rocks we worked our way toward shore and watched in horror when our friends' canoe overturned, tossing Jake and Ethel into the drink. Petrified, Linny and I clambered out of our canoe into chest-deep water. The rocks were really slippery as we inched our way along, rock by rock, dragging our vessel with us.

The sky was getting ominously dark when we finally passed the rapids and got back into our canoe. We heard the distant rumble of thunder and the sound of approaching rain. The skies opened up and water came down in buckets as lightning flashed in the distance. The peak of my baseball cap acted like an awning, keeping the rain out of my eyes and providing an interesting visual effect, which also kept my mind off the fact that the lightning seemed to be coming closer.

Bella and Nancy were paddling alongside us, and that was comforting, since everyone else had disappeared from sight. The rain had started to peter out when we saw a line of rocks ahead that appeared to span the waters from bank to bank. Paddling furiously in reverse we managed to slow down enough to head toward shore, where we promptly overturned both canoes. The water here was shallow, so Nancy was able to run after our life preservers which were floating lazily downstream. (Yes, I know we should have been wearing them.) She managed to snare all four and Jenny captured the paddles, while Linny and I tried to upright the canoes. Impossible! They were just too heavy. What were we going to do now?

As we contemplated our situation, two more canoes came into view, with four guys cruising down the river, singing and waving beer bottles. Linny began to weep extravagantly. Just so you know, this was a ploy. It was pathetic, but it worked. The gentlemen pulled over, got out of their canoes, and turned ours right side up. They wanted to give us some beer, probably figuring we could use a little artificial cheer, but we were too tired to even think about it. Back in the canoe, as it began to occur to us that this wasn't fun anymore, we turned the bend to find a welcoming committee cheering us to shore.

The rain started again while we were beaching our canoes. Linny and I ran for the showers hoping to warm up, and on the way out we were surprised to meet a friend who was there with her family. "Can we drive home with you?" we begged. "Sure," she said. Was that serendipity, or what? Angelic intervention? Who cared! We were saved! We headed straight for the barbeque, where Pastor Chris was dishing up hotdogs and burgers. Linny and I told him we were going home. In fact, what we said was, "We will never, ever again go on another canoe trip! And we're leaving right now. Don't anyone try to stop us!"

A week later, when my scrapes and bruises had begun to fade, my friend Chuck called and said he knew I had been wanting to go tubing (another adventure, since removed, on my bucket list) and he had decided to take his kids Upstate to give it a try. Wouldn't I like to go along? I enjoyed Chuck's company, and I liked his kids a lot, so I accepted. After hanging up the phone I smacked myself in the head. "What are you? Nuts? Is there no end to the punishment you're willing to inflict on yourself?"

Chuck was excited; the kids were excited; I was in a panic. When we reached the tubing site we looked down at a roiling river. "Oh God," I thought, "what have I done?" Chuck conferred with the keeper of the tubes, patted his five-year-old on the head, and said, "It's too dangerous. I'm sorry, but we're not going." So we all went out for a nice dinner and my days on the river were over for good!

* * *

FINDING MARTIN LUTHER

I grew up in Brooklyn on a street that peaked at Sixth Avenue and ran downhill towards Seventh. Standing in the middle of the street on Sixth we could see the Narrows, and I often went to bed at night with the mellow sound of fog horns singing me to sleep.

The upper half of the block was the turf of the Irish Catholic kids who almost all went to the school run by our neighborhood Catholic Church. The lower half was populated by a whole lot of Scandinavian Lutherans and members of a fundamentalist congregation, all of whom attended public school. There was some tension between the "publics" and the "privates" when school started in the fall, but for the most part we got along very well.

As an only child I treasured my friends and loved to spend time at Kitty's house, where every Sunday evening the whole family gathered to listen to Bishop Fulton J. Sheen on the radio. Kitty's mom had a serious desire to convert me to Catholicism, and her dream might have come true.

Kitty was thinking (at age 10) of becoming a nun, and she always took me with her on her excursions to local convents where she spoke seriously with the sisters about her ambitions. They all loved to see her, and when they found out that I was a Protestant, I think they liked to see me even more. We always had lovely cookies and milk while we visited, and I acquired several strings of rosary beads along the way.

I had started Sunday School at the Swedish Lutheran Church when I was about five years old. My father would take me on the trolley from our house which, at that time, was on Bay 31st Street in the Bensonhurst area. I loved Sunday School from the first moment, and when we sang "Jesus Loves Me" I knew the song was just for me.

I never knew where my father was while I was in Sunday School. He was certainly not in church. He had no use for it himself, but he and my mother decided it was necessary for me to learn the Lutheran faith that they had chosen to ignore in their new homeland. Years later my cousin told me that our dads used to meet in the local saloon while we were learning the commandments, but she may have been pulling my leg. I was a very gullible kid and will even today believe most of what you tell me unless you're clearly making it up.

What distracted me from Martin Luther was the lower sanctuary at the Catholic Church. It was dark and resembled what I imagined a grotto would look like, having been especially impressed by the movie "The Song of Bernadette." It smelled wonderful! And I couldn't take my eyes away from all the beautiful candles burning at the various altars.

I sat in that beautiful place of worship many, many Saturdays, as Kitty was obsessive about going to confession every week. I would sit in the first pew near the confessional sniffing the incense, delighting in the glow of altar candles and votive lights, just immersing myself in the whole experience, while Kitty waited on line with the adults and children who waited on the priests.

Even though I enjoyed myself immensely I did wonder what Kitty had to confess as we spent quite a lot of time together after school and she always seemed like a good girl to me. When I came home I would beseech my mother to let me become a Catholic. I wanted that experience to belong to me, too.

My parents were not prejudiced in any sense and got along with the neighbors of every persuasion. They were also very easy with me, letting me do all kinds of things that my own son would never permit his children to do. But that was too much. My mother had a deep fear of anything Catholic and, in retrospect, I must have given her a lot of grief about this, but she promised me that if I still wanted to convert after my Confirmation, she would not object, and would even support my decision in the face of my father's disapproval.

My mother was a wise woman. She bided her time and when I was 13 and Confirmation classes began she encouraged me to go to all the social gatherings as well, and I soon forgot that I had considered becoming a deserter. In the meantime, Kitty had discovered boys in her own milieu and our friendship petered out, although I did attend a few Confraternity dances with her at her church. We Lutherans weren't allowed to dance in our Fellowship Hall lest the devil find us and overcome us with unhealthy desires, but I always loved to dance.

Around this time my parents decided that church was okay after all, and they went twice a year: on Easter, and at 5 a.m. on Christmas morning, when Christmas was honored by a special celebratory worship service in the Swedish language, just as it was done in the Old Country.

So that's how I found Martin Luther again. And I've been a big fan of his ever since.

* * *

CROSSWORD PUZZLES

I became fascinated with crossword puzzles after retiring (for the first time) in 2000. I rarely had time for them before that, and for years I kept getting the terms crossword and jigsaw confused. My friend Barbara, who lives in Florida, likes the crosswords as much as I do, so when I head south to visit her, she makes a copy of the daily puzzle and we sit out on the lanai with cold drinks, put our collective feet up and puzzle away.

My friend Phil in New Jersey enjoys it when we work the puzzle together. He often guesses the complete word from the letters available before I get a chance to tell him the clue. (He's very smart!) His wife, Lora, is delighted that we have this "thing" in common since while we're busy wording she gets to do whatever she needs to without any interference from us.

Lately I've been wondering: when I'm working a puzzle, how much cheating is allowed? The Sunday puzzle in the local newspaper is often quite difficult, and the solution is printed within a page or two of the puzzle itself. How tempting it is to look up a few words when I get stuck. So is this a moral issue, or what?

Cheating *is* bad/wrong/unacceptable, but does that apply to crossword puzzles? Let's get real here. Does my cheating on the puzzle amount to the same thing as writing my son's college papers for him (Just for the record I never did that, but a friend of mine did.)? Is it the same as cheating on one's income tax, or on one's spouse?

The question was called at Christmas when Lora gave me an electronic crossword puzzle solver. Electronics are a massive challenge for me, so it took me a week or so to figure out how to turn it on. After that it was a quick jump of two or three weeks more to learn how to find the word I was looking for. Not that the little machine always comes through. It has said, "sorry, can't help," more than once. I'm not by nature a violent person, but sometimes it makes me so frustrated that I want to throw it against the wall and stomp on it when it bounces back. So my conclusion about cheating is, it's more trouble than it's worth with crossword puzzles, and when I cheat I'm really cheating on myself anyway. I'll just let the morality chips fall where they may.

But I digress. What I wanted to say about working puzzles is how intriguing words are. The other day I found myself in a lengthy meditation about the word "mature." "Mature" was the clue, and the meaning they were looking for was "ripe." This conjured up several different ideas. What about "ripe for adventure?" Now at my stage of maturity, "ripe for adventure" hardly seems likely, but it does sound exciting and definitely appealing.

Thinking about "ripe" in terms of fruit, however, is just a short jump to "over-ripe" which might also be interpreted as "on the edge of rotting." I refuse to allow my matureness to be thought of that way!

"Ripe for the picking" is a phrase we've heard often enough. If we equate that with "mature" are we thinking of the old folks who have been scammed because they were "ripe for the picking?" Or could it mean that in our maturity we are so desirable that we have become "ripe for the picking," if, by chance, someone were looking to make a choice?

My dictionary added two more definitions that really appealed to me. One is "fully or highly developed," which could lead in a lot of different directions. But my absolute favorite definition is "perfected." Isn't it lovely to know we have finally reached the state of perfection?

I could go on like this, but I'm sure you get the point. Words are fun, and thinking about them is good for the mature, ripe, perfected brain. So let's all get busy with the crossword puzzles and help our brains to keep on ripening in the best possible way!

And try not to cheat.

* * *

UNHINGED BY TECHNOLOGY

People keep telling me that my world will be open to endless possibilities when I finally get an iPhone. The instrument does look very appealing. I like the idea of just sweeping my finger across the screen and getting all kinds of interesting information. Its owner looks very smart and sophisticated, and I'm all for that. The trouble is, I'm inept. My head just doesn't work that way.

When cell phones first came out, I resisted. My son finally insisted and put me on his family plan where I remained for several years, paying a minimum fee for something I rarely ever used. If the phone rang, which it seldom did, I ignored it. None of my friends had one, and I figured I wouldn't want to hear from anyone who did have my number.

Eventually I decided that the stars were aligned properly with the planets and it was time to get with the program, so I took the phone with me to work, about 25 miles from home, thinking that if I got stuck on the Long Island Expressway for a couple of days I would be able to call Ed and tell him I'd be late for dinner.

One evening it was my turn to staff the hotline. Three other counselors were staying late to see clients, but we had a break around 5 p.m. when no one was expected. The office phones were turned off during evening hours, except for the hotline, and we couldn't make personal calls there, so I decided to call Ed from my cell phone. He wasn't home, so I left a message asking him to call me back. The problem was, I knew how to call out, but I didn't know how to answer the phone. I know this sounds ridiculous, but that's the way it was.

The phone rang and rang, and I didn't know what to do with it! I figured Ed would try again, since I hadn't known how to set up the voice mail anyway, and I went looking for my coworkers who were enjoying a little quiet time in the break room. "Help!" I said. "Ed is going to call and I don't know how to answer the phone." At that moment the phone rang again and, as it turned out, no one else knew how to answer it either. So there we were, four people with Master's degrees, and not one of us knew how to answer the damn phone!

Well, I finally did figure it out, and some time later, feeling just a little too cocky, decided I needed a better phone. For what reason I'm not sure, since I still rarely used it. When I brought it to my son, once again, to have him set it up for me, I sat out on their porch enjoying the fall breezes. About an hour passed; the phone was still inside, and I was still outside. What had happened to it? A look through the front window told the story. My five-year-old grandson was playing games on it! Did I know it had games? Don't ask.

The situation hasn't improved much since then. In fact, I'm less proficient after the passage of 14 years. I resented the cost of the service which I rarely use, so I decided to get a GoPhone from the AT+T store nearby. The cost is minimal, but …. the phone rang and I hadn't used it in so long that I had forgotten, again, how to answer it. I considered the possibly this might be a genetic disability, since my second son recently purchased the most up-to-date phone available and admitted that he wasn't able to answer that one! Fortunately both of us have gotten our acts together. As it turned out, David's phone had a defect which needed some kind of adjustment, but I had to go back to the store (feeling really dumb) for professional assistance.

Don't ask me how I managed to get this story written. The computer has been doing very strange things, like indenting whole paragraphs without any input from me, and refusing to write the letter "T," or anything else for that matter. It also changed the size to something huge …. all by itself! I had to turn everything off and start from scratch, but, finally, here it is. Now that it's done, I sincerely hope it's worth it.

By the way, if you need to call me, please use the land line.

* * *

WORDS TO LIVE BY?

As the years have passed I've come to realize that a few catch phrases could sum up my personal philosophy of life. I'm not sure if this is a good or a bad thing, but there seems to be great wisdom on the front of a lot of tee shirts if we just take a minute to think about it.

When I was in high school a million years ago a friend gave me a little wallet card that declared, "My mind is made up! Don't confuse me with the facts." I carried that card around for more years than I can count, but the implications never grew old. In the presidential election of 2012 I threw the sentiment around freely to some of my politically wrong-headed friends, but I don't think they took the hint. And though the card itself is long gone, I often think of the phrase as a touchstone when I find myself getting adamant about something or other.

The next significant saying that comes to mind is the one I heard back in the '60s when I was beginning to realize I'm a feminist: "A woman needs a man like a fish needs a bicycle." Anyone who knows me well is quite aware that this is not my personal take on male-female relationships. But it was fuel for the fire that had been sparked in me by our family doctor who posited that the root of my anxieties was too much intellectual energy and no place to put it.

Twenty years later and finally admitting that I could only retain my sanity by getting a divorce, I was given a pretty little poster by my friend Linny, showing a tiny kitten with huge blue eyes and a terrified expression clinging frantically to a thin tree branch. Underneath the crazy kitty were the words, "Lord, save me from myself."

Linny knew me well. Newly single and feeling 18 years old again, I was less cautious than I had been during the years I was responsible for everything in my life, including husband (gone), children (grown and moved out) and home. The sense of adventure and endless possibilities I experienced by making the decision to end it after years of feeling depressed and worthless led me down a lot of interesting paths. When I internalized, at last, that it was necessary to cut the marital tie I was pretty sure I was stepping off a cliff. How exhilarating to discover that I could fly!

Some of the things I might have missed had I not abandoned my usual caution were really good, and some not so much, but nothing was fatal and I learned a lot about myself along the way. The good ones have been too numerous to list. The worst was a trip to Eastern Europe with a charming ex-pat who turned out to be the poster child for the term "Ugly American" the minute his toes touched the pavement in Vienna. But that's another story, and I'm still here to tell it, if ever I decide that I want to.

As retirement approached, the words that resonated with me were: "The Golden Years." So far, I've found those words to be mostly true.
What a sense of freedom to retire in 2000 and return to work four times just because I felt like it.

My first post-work job was as a bridal shop salesperson. What a kick, being surrounded by beautiful gowns, lace and tulle. And how nice were the grateful parents of prom girls who trusted me to keep the kids out of the slinky, sexy numbers they gravitated toward the minute they walked in the door.

Two more part-time returns were to the domestic violence agency from which I had originally retired, and the last was to serve as pastoral assistant at my church during our anticipated one-year interim period, which turned into almost four years. Besides feeling useful, I had fun being surrounded by 30, 40 and 50 year-olds who kept me feeling young and up to date. These were certainly some of "The Golden Years" for me, and I am grateful to have had them.

Now that I'm savoring my time at Lutherburgh I occasionally find myself over-extended, but the phrase that keeps me moving is "Pay It Forward." I'm pretty sure that if I live long enough, I will be one of the folks who remain here due to the kindness of others, so while I'm able to get around and go and do I will, feeling sure that others will do the same when I can't manage it anymore.

Recently I came across a new catch-phrase that strikes me as useful in anyone's life: "Be Yourself! Everyone else is taken." That's profound when you give it some thought, and it sums up several years of therapy for me.

But probably the most significant phrases in my life are variations on a theme that I've heard from childhood: "What does the law require of you but to do justice, and to love kindness, and to walk humbly with your God?" (Micah 6:8).

No doubt in my mind; these are truly "Words to Live By!"

* * *

CONFIRMATION CLASS

I was really looking forward to Confirmation Class. I had started Sunday School early, so it wasn't as though I didn't know what was coming. It would be hard to learn everything, but then again, it meant I was growing up.

When I was five years old we lived quite a distance away from the Swedish Lutheran Church in Brooklyn, New York, so on Sunday mornings my father would take me on the trolley car all the way from Bensonhurst to Bay Ridge to attend Sunday School. The ride itself was exciting enough, but I was overjoyed to learn that "Jesus Loves Me." I don't know where my dad went for the hour I was sponging up kid theology, but I am sure he wasn't in church. My parents almost never went to church themselves. When I was about seven we moved to Bay Ridge, a mile or so from the church, and by the time I was ten I was walking to church by myself.

Just before we were to start Confirmation lessons, Cindy arrived. I was fascinated and shocked to see her wearing lipstick to Sunday School. Wow! What guts! It was Tangee Natural, and I can even remember what it tasted like, because the next time I had enough pennies I ran to the Five and Ten Cent Store to buy some of my own, which I then had to hide from my mother.

I knew who my best friend was going to be. Cindy was ready for anything, and I passionately wanted that vibe for myself, even though I had no clue what "anything" might turn out to be. Both of us were only children, and we both missed having a sibling, so we became sisters by design.

Confirmation Class was going to be a blessing in so many ways! I would be going someplace where I could meet *boys*. My parents had decided that I would be best off attending an all-girls New York City school, so I had no way of meeting any boys except for a few in the neighborhood who weren't very appealing; I had known them for too long to find them interesting. I had been pestering my mother for years to get me an older brother who could introduce me to his friends, but she never obliged so Confirmation Class seemed ideal for my purposes.

There were about 25 kids in my class, and we were really more interested in each other than we were in the Small Catechism. We got into the habit of gathering at the nearby ice cream parlor after class, where we drank gallons of coffee, which was lots cheaper than ice cream. If one added enough milk, sugar, and imagination it could pass for something more exciting, so we didn't feel deprived.

We were acquiring friendships that would last forever, and we were learning how to be with each other in same and opposite-sex friendships. So while we studied for the dreaded Overhearing that was to come, when family and church members would watch us stumble through recitations of the meaning of the Ten Commandments and the Apostles' Creed according to Martin Luther, we had lots of fun together.

Did we really learn anything about Confirmation, you may ask? Well, of course we did! We learned that dancing was not allowed because it might lead to "other things," which we were more than eager to learn about. Pastor Hanson was about 96 years old at the time, and he had a tendency to fall asleep during class. He always woke with a start when we digressed from the Catechism. It was as if he were wired for Luther, and anything else rang his alarm bell.

Confirmation Day finally arrived, and we all knelt at the altar rail. The boys looked awesome in their dark suits and ties, and we girls were in various stages of embarrassment in our long white dresses and white gloves. It was, finally, after three long years, almost over. Except that now we would have to start preparing for our first Holy Communion!

Confirmation Girls (author second from right)

* * *

Confirmation Portrait

Author, age 13

GETTING FROM HERE TO THERE

Lately I've been thinking about how it will feel when I finally decide to stop driving and get rid of my car. The words I always hear from friends are, "I don't want to give up my independence." That's a definite downer, but on the other hand relinquishing car ownership will leave me with quite a bit more discretionary income, and I will be able to stop worrying about crashing into things, or worse yet, people, if I suffer a lapse in judgment or some kind of physical problem while driving.

While I was working as a counselor at a Senior Center on Long Island I met a delightful woman, Elsa, who wanted to discuss that very subject. It seems that she had had a few minor "dents and dings" as she described it to me, and just that morning she had driven too close to a parked car and "happened" to take the driver's side mirror away with her. She was too embarrassed to stop, she told me, and had been praying for a way to make up for it.

Well, atonement aside, I steered the conversation to her options. She admitted that she had been thinking of giving her car to her grandson, so that was one option. The Center was in an affluent neighborhood, and my client was always very well dressed, so I inquired if she had the means to take taxis if necessary. "Oh, yes," she said. "That wouldn't be any problem at all." And, she offered, her daughter would take her anywhere she wanted to go. Well, that sounded like a no-brainer to me, and she seemed to agree. As she picked herself up to leave she said, "I'm going to tell my daughter when I see her today that Kevin can have my car.

I think it's time for me to stop driving."

I drove the 25 miles home that afternoon figuratively patting myself on the back all the way. Was I a great counselor, or what? I was getting Elsa off the road and making her entire town safer for motorists, cyclists and pedestrians. Good for me!

I didn't see Elsa again for several weeks, and when she breezed into the Center I asked her how it was going without her car. "Oh," she said, "My daughter told me I'm still a good driver, so I decided to keep on going for a while longer."

I'm not sure which old adage applies here. Is it "don't count your chickens" or "never trust anyone over 30?" Anyway, I learned that back pats can turn into butt kicks within seconds. I also found myself deeply skeptical about the daughter's motives. Did she see a life for herself in which she drove her mom on endless rounds from one shop to another and from doctor's appointment to doctor's appointment? Maybe she saw dollar bills floating away through taxi windows. I don't know and never will, but with Elsa on the road I fear for the population of her town and the rest of Long Island as well.

It seems that getting from one place to another has an emotional context as well as a physical one. How do we get from the place where we are to where we want to go? Or on a philosophical level, where *do* we want to go? I suspect that the issue of driving is so deeply ingrained in many of us that we see ourselves as "less than" once the car has disappeared over the hill ….. and we've gone over the hill with it!

You've probably already figured out that I haven't, yet, given up driving. I recently heard that one of our neighbors has an interesting idea. He says he'll stop driving the next time (heaven forbid!) he has an accident …. but only if he was the person who caused it.

I'm not sure I buy that, but it's always good to have a plan!

* * *

YOU CAN'T MAKE THIS STUFF UP!

My friend Barbara is NUTS about shoes. On many of our shopping trips together she has come home with five or six pairs, and when I want to tease her I call her "The Imelda Marcos of Tampa.' When she moved to Florida eight years ago, she took more than 100 pairs of shoes with her, and I know that many more have been added to her collection since then. Sadly, Barbara hasn't been feeling too well lately and she will readily admit to being depressed about it when we talk on the phone.

So one Friday morning, as I was checking out the merchandise in the Lutherburgh Gift Shop, I came upon a coffee mug that was calling Barbara's name. This cup was oversized, bright green, and had a stylish woman painted on it with the words, "All I want for Christmas is world peace, happiness, and a pair of cute shoes." I decided to buy it for Barbara and send it down to Florida to cheer her up. How could she not perk up with such a perfect cup for her morning joe? Best of all, the cup must have been donated to the gift shop, because the price was 25 cents, plus 2 cents tax, for a grand total of 27 cents. I could act like the world's best friend …. and for a minimal financial investment! What could be better!

As soon as I got home I wrote a cheery little note and stuffed it into the cup, then found some squooshed up, heavy-duty paper in my desk drawer and padded the cup inside and out. Too lazy to walk to the shopping center just a block away, I climbed into my car and took off. The trouble was, I was feeling guilty about not walking, so I decided to park south of the market and walk across the parking lot to the postal store and get some exercise while doing my good deed.

The store clerk was happy to package the cup for me and rolled it abundantly in bubble wrap held in place with a lot of scotch tape. I hadn't thought to ask what the price would be, so when the clerk handed me the receipt, I was bemused by the numbers: $2.50 for the packaging, $11.25 for parcel post, and 15 cents tax for a grand total of $13.90! Percentage-wise, I could have bought a plane ticket and delivered it in person!

"What the heck," I thought. It would remind Barbara that there are people who love her, and that's always a cheerful thought. So I paid the man and headed out to the parking lot to hike back to my car. There weren't many cars in the lot that morning, and as I was strolling back I happened to look down. There was money on the ground. Not coins, but a dollar bill! Wow! The most money I've ever found on the street has been a quarter, and here was a whole dollar.

"Aha," I thought. "The universe is rewarding me for doing a good deed." But, guess what? It was a $20 bill! I couldn't believe it …. I had spent more to send that package than made any sense in any universe and gotten back $6.10 more than I had spent, within a matter of only minutes. Had I stumbled onto some new system of investing?

I stood there, mesmerized, for a few seconds, pondering whether I could find the person who had lost the money. But it was impossible to guess where that person might be. Was he in one of the stores? Had she dropped it when she put her packages in her car? So, of course, I decided it was meant to be mine and that I should keep it.

Now if you come and tell me that was your $20 I found, you will be out of luck. I was so pleased with myself that I went to the State store and bought a bottle of vodka.

* * *

ADDENDUM: ANOTHER TRUE STORY

Here's another one. On Friday I was supposed to make reservations for dinner, and of course I forgot. When my friend came into the Gift Shop where I was volunteering that morning she reminded me, and I said I would do it on the way back to my apartment. It was such a nice day that I deviated from the original plan and decided to walk home outdoors, and, again, forgot about making the reservation.

When I reached the entrance near the Belvedere building awning, I noticed a piece of paper on the ground. Hey, last time I found $20, but this was just a sheet of paper. I thought I would be a good citizen, pick it up and throw it away, but first I looked at the handwritten message. It said, "Call the dining room."

You can't make this stuff up!

* * *

STRESS RELIEF

It seems to me that "stress" became a popular word sometime around the l970s. Perhaps it was a reaction to the funky '60s, when everyone was invited to do their own thing and not worry about convention, duty or how your parents raised you. So when we all came down from doing our things, we realized that we were now stressed out from the consequences.

If society embraces a word and the concept it expresses, of course there must be a way to solve the problem, whatever it is. My feminist soul wants me to believe this must be attributable to the male point of view, which is usually "If it's broke, we have to fix it." (And sometimes, reading the news lately, "Even if it's not broke, we're going to fiddle with it anyway.")

So, how do we relieve our stress? Depending on one's age, the options vary. Young people who are under the drinking age have nevertheless occasionally chosen to get blasted with beer, delivered through a tube from an overhead keg straight to the gullet. I read about this in a popular magazine. We seniors more politely meet for a glass (or two or three) of wine before dinner. And for those who are able, recent magazine articles tell us that sex is a great stress reliever, but I'm not going to go there.

Some of us enjoy jigsaw and crossword puzzles that carry our brains off in challenging directions. While relieving stress, these pursuits can also create stress by reminding us that we didn't used to have to look up the words, and where is that darn dictionary anyhow?

There are still some people who think that coffee and a cigarette will relieve their stress. This works when one is in need of instant gratification, but how stressful is it to look at pictures of ravaged lungs and oral cancer as those spoilsports in the health care industry want us to do? And let's not mention the overeating …. (cookies, cookies, chocolate, please!), also good for the moment but, as the old adage goes, "a taste on the lips, straight to the hips."

So I'm here to tell you that I have found the PERFECT stress reliever, although it's only good for decent weather …. no rain, no snow, but clouds are just fine. It's …. are you ready for this? …. blowing bubbles!

I challenge you to try it.

Go to the dollar store and get a big bottle of bubble stuff. Then go outdoors and pucker up. This will cost you almost nothing, and I have not yet discovered a single health problem that arises from it. You can enjoy this activity all by yourself (though like most things in life I think it's more fun to do with a friend), and you can do it standing up or sitting down. Personally, I think it's better here at Lutherburgh if you can do it from a balcony, but patio sitters can have fun with bubbles, too.

If you are too bashful to attempt this on your own, (after all, someone might see you) just come by the Belvedere building awning on a late afternoon, look up to the third floor, and you may find me hanging over my balcony railing, bubble stuff in hand, sending bubbles out into the universe.

If you holler loud enough to get my attention, I'll invite you up to give it a try. No charge for the bubble stuff.

* * *

DANCING

For as long as I can remember I've enjoyed dancing, even when I haven't known what I was doing …. possibly even more when I didn't know what I was doing.

My mother was an avid movie-goer, but my father had no interest whatsoever, so she would take me with her to a matinee even when I was very young. Those were the days when musicals were the rage, and we always had to see everything in which Sonia Henie starred. She was Norwegian, but we could forgive the fact that she wasn't Swedish because she was such a great ice skater. My mother told me that when we returned home after watching Sonia Henie tear up the ice I would attach blocks to the bottoms of my feet with rubber bands and "skate" on the kitchen floor. Flops and bruises counted for nothing compared to the joy of being Sonia Henie!

Before we moved to Bay Ridge, Brooklyn, we lived in Bensonhurst in a three-story wooden mansion which had been the summer home of a wealthy family. It had been purchased and renovated by the local Republican Club. My dad took care of the property and we lived in the third-floor apartment that had been the nursery. The house had two huge rooms on the ground floor, and on weekends our relatives would come to visit and we would play Swedish music on the Victrola and dance the afternoons away.

I was always so happy when my uncle would invite me to dance the *hambo* with him. It required some fancy footwork for a little kid, with a dip and a hop, and my uncle would whirl me around until I thought I was flying. Not so long ago my old friend Max and I decided to see if we could still ace the *hambo*. His wife looked dubious, but she didn't object. When Max dipped and I hopped his knee went out and I fell over. So much for youthful enthusiasm in the elderly!

When we moved to Bay Ridge some of the neighbor girls were learning Irish step dancing and we would gather near the front stoop and jump up and down with lots of energy, if no skill. Dancing in the living room of our four-room apartment was a challenge. When the family came over we did dance, but only two couples at a time could attempt it, and careful navigating was essential.

About that time my mom enrolled me in a Swedish children's dance club where we learned the traditional folk dances and went out to festivals and performances to show that the Old Country hadn't been entirely overcome by American culture. At a performance at City Center one year, the guest star was Christine Jorgensen. My sweet prudish mom, who as far as I know never uttered the word "sex" out loud, was almost out of her mind trying to explain why this person was a celebrity.

I lost interest in the dance club when I started Confirmation classes and met some boys and girls who also knew many of the Swedish dances I had learned. When classes were over and we graduated to Junior Fellowship League we would party and dance at each other's homes. The dance of the day was the Lindy, and we bounced around for hours on end, with an occasional slow dance and schottische thrown in.

The best Swedish dances were held at Vasa Castle Hall in the Bronx, and on Saturday nights five or six of us girls would get all dressed up and ride the subway from Brooklyn to dance ourselves into a state of exhaustion. In those days we could ride the subway home at 3 a.m. and not think a thing about it. Sometimes, if we were lucky, we would meet someone who had come up by car and we could jam ourselves into the back seat for a more comfortable (?) ride home.

When my husband and I moved to Long Island we lived in a brand-new housing development. Our civic association sponsored dances at the firehouse, and my parents would drive out from Brooklyn to baby sit so we could attend. Later we became more involved with church friends, but they also loved to dance, so we were back to the house parties, but with a new crowd. Unassuming Jenna, who could get crocked on one glass of wine, was inspired to dance on the coffee table if properly encouraged.   In church the next day she would blush endearingly when someone teased her about it. To this day my son tells anyone who will listen that his sleep was constantly disturbed by the sounds of Trini Lopez and ice rattling around in glassware. All I can say to that is, "get over it, kid."

Just recently I got my first-ever pair of tap shoes! One of the members of our tap class told us that when she was a child her tap teacher called her parents to tell them they were wasting their money. This class is her answer to that! She's doing well, so maybe it's just more fun when you're a grownup.

I may be in my eighties, but who says I have to act my age? These days at Lutherburgh you will find me trotting around at parties trying to find someone to dance with. Gentlemen, I warn you that I am relentless. Even so, I haven't had much success, but you all are probably the better for it.

* * *

BATHROOM TISSUE

Please notice that I've titled this reflection in politically correct language so as to preserve all our delicate sensibilities. But I'm really talking about good old-fashioned toilet paper here, so you might as well know that from the beginning.

The other morning as I was reading my favorite health and wellness magazine I came across an ad that captured my attention immediately. Here was a little sprig of green leaves growing out of the center of a toilet paper roll! The headline said, "Help save two million trees without even noticing."

This reminded me of a TV commercial I had seen many times in which hundreds, or possibly thousands, of toilet paper tubes were careening through the canyons of New York City, with the startling voice-over announcement that the paper company was preparing to market rolls of toilet paper without ….. (tah dah!) card board tubes in the center.

"Why," I wondered to myself, "is this such a big deal?" I mean, who really cares, except possibly scores of kindergarten and Vacation Bible School teachers who rely on them to construct various esoteric and frequently useless projects.

Well, I got a coupon in the mail for $1.00 off six or more rolls and made my way to the supermarket to see what the fuss was all about. What I discovered was, first, that the new and improved version they carried only came in packages of four, so in order to use my coupon I would have to buy two packages. I also learned that the new product, with the card board tube missing, costs more than the old stuff that has the tube.

How come, when they take something AWAY from the product, it gets more expensive rather than less? Shouldn't a roll of toilet paper without a card board tube be cheaper to make? Will the extra cost for the "improved" product ever make up for the cost of ads in pricey magazines and the commercial air time?

That got me thinking of a story a friend told me about toilet paper. She said that her father, a native-born American of good German stock, always insisted on rationing the toilet paper. When she and her brother were quite young her dad, when he was at home, would stand at the bathroom door and issue three squares per person to whomever entered the room. I found that terrifying, but I have since told that story to others and they have said they experienced something similar.

As a person who cannot relax without knowing that there are at least six rolls in a nearby closet, or perhaps under the bed since closet space is so limited in my apartment, I cannot imagine what three squares of tissue could possibly do for any living human being. I have learned to cope with limited storage space by keeping large quantities of toilet paper in the trunk of my car. The only problem that can arise with that arrangement is if I should run out in the middle of a snowstorm and have to resurrect my old boots and brave the elements to take care of business. One does what one has to do.

My friend said they learned to manage on three little sheets of paper out of necessity, but the day after she returned from her honeymoon she ran to the store and bought 25 rolls.

Well, considering that cave people didn't have this modern advantage, and during wars and depressions old newspapers filled the bill, I suppose I have nothing to complain about.

I don't have to forage for big oak leaves or keep stacks of old newspapers in the bathroom.

It's good to be able to appreciate the simple pleasures of life!

* * *

GARDENING

Keeping a garden was a very small blip on my radar during my growing up years in Brooklyn. Until I was about seven we lived in a house with a yard, and my father was happy raising his favorite flowers along the fence that separated us from our neighbor, a sweet, grey-haired old lady who would sneak out at night and steal them. Even when my dad caught her red-handed she insisted that the stems she took were broken and she was just helping to clean up the flower beds. My dad gave up on flowers shortly thereafter, when we moved to a four-room apartment on a block that was greened solely by a few scrawny curbside trees.

Later, when I married and our little family moved to Long Island, I was overjoyed to have a real backyard with real grass and some space to plant things, like the two tiny lilac bushes I nurtured in coffee cans on our apartment kitchen windowsill for almost a year before our house was built.

Although my husband had spent his childhood summers at a cottage in New Jersey where his dad grew those lilacs, as well as spectacular tomatoes, our early efforts at gardening were mixed. Of course we had to grow tomatoes and we had success with them. But our first attempt at expanding the garden was a "cornfield" consisting of one row along our neighbor's fence, planted to please the children, which produced only two pitiful-looking, pale beige ears and a few saggy stalks. David, about 4 years old at the time, insisted that I cook the corn, but once they were on his plate his discerning palate took over and both ears went untouched into the garbage. Steve, being older and wiser, wanted nothing to do with that corn from the first minute he saw it.

As time went on we became more proficient at our gardening chores, and we were always ready to try something new. One year, after we had planted a tasteful grouping of hemlocks along the side of our patio, intended to grow into a privacy fence, a friend told us of the wonderful results he was having in his garden with chicken manure. He neglected to tell us that he put this into a tub of water at the back of his property and drew a small amount out from time to time to water his vegetable garden.

My husband, in a burst of enthusiasm but without getting the details, went out and got some chicken manure from someplace and distributed gobs of it around the base of each hemlock, watering it into deep pools of pooh. Sometime around noon the next day, when the full sun had hit the patio, I went out to hang the wash and could hardly get my breath! Anyone who has been a farmer would have known to expect the stench, but it was a shock to us. We couldn't sit on our patio for several weeks after that.

Gardening became a chore I had no time for when I began to live by myself. The flowers and tomatoes disappeared. The shrubs and trees were badly in need of grooming, and I had to pay a neighborhood teen to mow the lawn. Later, when Ed and I decided to move in together, he was tending lawns and trimming shrubs at both houses, so I sold mine and decided to be a gardener again at his place. Ed was into vegetables. Oh, joy!

Fresh tomatoes again! He was really happy to have someone help him in his garden, and I was thrilled to learn from an expert.

Have you ever experienced the delight of seeing no zucchini one day, and finding a 6-inch long one under a leaf on the next? Every day in our garden was an adventure!

We had a large corner yard and I determined to plant all kinds of beautiful flowers along the fence to delight the neighbors as well as myself. Before I moved in I was cleaning out closets and found, brilliantly painted in shades of red, blue and gold, a three-foot high plaster statue of the Sacred Heart of Jesus stashed away in a corner. Ed's late wife had been a devout woman, so I could understand why it was in the house; I also understood why it was tucked away in the back of the closet.

Jesus in Our Garden

This was a dilemma. What does one do with such a thing? I didn't feel comfortable throwing it in the trash since it was Jesus, after all, but neither was I ready to put it on display in the house. My solution turned out to be the flower garden, where it stood for several years, slowly eroding in the wind and weather, until it quietly melted away into the soil from whence it had come.

Now at Lutherburgh I enjoy the little potted-flower garden that I've planted on my balcony. The Black Eyed Susan vine will grow as far as I'll let it, literally inches overnight. It can be trained, but I have to be vigilant. Last year I joked with my dinner companions that, if I didn't show up some evening, they should come upstairs to see if I needed to be cut loose from the greenery.

The Great Big Vine

Best of all, when I last visited the garden center I was seduced by a gorgeous, dark green tomato plant and had to take it home with me. Oh, joy! Fresh tomatoes again! I hope!

* * *

PEA SOUP IS FOREVER

There was a time when I was a good cook. For years and years I happily basted, mashed and glazed my way through Thanksgiving dinners, forming the butter into little turkeys and making biscuits from scratch. At Christmastime I prepared my own version of Swedish Smorgasbord, always omitting lutefisk, a disgusting fish "delicacy" which some irreverent Swede has called "the piece of cod that passes all understanding" and which I personally consider to be unfit for human consumption. As a single woman I enjoyed hosting groups of both single and married friends for impromptu dinners and planned BBQs, and when Ed and I decided to become a couple, we hosted lots of parties for family and friends. Later, in my job as Pastoral Assistant, I often prepared dinners for various church committees just for fun.

I do miss cooking, even though I'm delighted to enjoy my dinner after a walk down the hall to the Lutherburgh dining room, not having to touch a pot along the way. So when my friend Barbara said she was coming from her home in Florida to visit me I knew it was time to make our favorite dish, pea soup. I hadn't done this in a *very* long time, but I thought (as I often do) "How hard could it be?"

The supermarket had several kinds of beans for soup-making, and they all came with recipes on the packages, so that was easy: just pick up some carrots and onions and a chunk of ham and go to it. Once home, I discovered that I didn't have any bouillon cubes, but I did have some beef base that tastes better anyway, and garlic and celery were already on hand. The only thing missing was a bay leaf, but I figured "What the heck," (as I often do) and went ahead without it.

The soup bubbled merrily away as I worked on a crossword puzzle until it was time to go to dinner then turned off the pot and went downstairs, figuring I could finish when I got back.

My apartment smelled divine when I returned, so I gave the soup another half-hour of simmer time while I unearthed the blender to puree some of the vegetable-laden liquid before returning it to the pot to finish. Just getting that together was a problem in itself, since my blender was in pieces in the cabinet next to the stove, mixed in with a food processor, a popcorn popper, various attachments, some refrigerator dishes and a few other things I didn't remember ever having. But I managed to assemble the blender and set it up on the counter next to the stove.

I carefully ladled in several cups of liquid, put the top on, and hit the "puree" button. Whoa! Volcanic eruption! Soup spout! Pea soup in motion in all directions! I did have one hand on the lid, but the force of the startup was too much for me. "Take your finger off the button, you dummy!" I yelled at myself. Which I did, but still, it was too late. Pea soup dripped from the bottom of the microwave, ran down the front of the oven, fried on the glass-top stove, glued itself to the front of the cabinet, hit the floor, covered my fair-trade garlic saver, ran inside the popcorn popper which stood beside the blender on the counter, and worst of all, hit the side of the refrigerator and slid down the space between the fridge and the counter, where, perhaps, some of it remains to this day.

Do you know what the trouble is with spilled pea soup? It doesn't remain liquid. It congeals into little bits of pasty stuff that feels like sand on the counters and doesn't want to wipe off. Pea soup had seeped into the little carved opening of the garlic saver and morphed into a cement-like substance. It was packed into the ridges of the stove and had to be dug out of the popcorn popper. The kitchen rugs went right into the washing machine, and all my modern plastic canisters with the metal latches were awash in pea-goop that eventually had to be removed with a toothpick.

My tiny kitchen needed a major cleanup and I did what was necessary. Thank goodness the housekeeping staff was due early the next morning! But I'm not giving up on cooking when the mood strikes, and after hearing this story, Barbara assured me that the soup was super-delicious, in fact mind-boggling, and definitely worth the effort.

* * *

A PLETHORA OF PASTORS

The other day it came to my attention that three more pastors had moved in to Lutherburgh. My goodness .... where did they all come from? Anyway, as I was counting pastors, assuming that I may have missed a stray Huguenot or two, it occurred to me that there ought to be a collective name for them, and "plethora" came immediately to mind, probably because of the nice sound of it. Unfortunately, although "plethora" mean "lots of" it also means "possibly too many," and that's *not* what I intend to convey!

Then I began to think about the names for groups of other things and discovered that collective words for animals, birds, and such are definitely worth a look. The place to go, as for so many other obscure and peculiar facts one might wish to discover, is the internet. What I found are a raft of plurals too good not to share.

Since I began this essay by counting pastors, I should mention that there are several collective words that ring a bell for those of us who attend places of worship from time to time. For example, both plovers and alligators in the aggregate are called "congregations." Picture the pastor standing before a collection of these two, preaching about peace, and watching some members of the congregation chewing up the other members! Whoop! I wouldn't want to sit in one of those pews.

More pleasing, I think, would be an "exaltation" or "ascension" of larks or, perhaps, a "wisdom" of wombats. What is a wombat, you may ask. The wombat is a short, robust, burrowing marsupial native to Australia. What makes them wise is not immediately evident, at least not to me.

Some collective names seem truly descriptive of the animals they are grouping: a "pounce" or "nuisance" of cats, depending on how fond of them you are; a "destruction" of cats in the wild; a "quiver" of cobras (the cobras may or may not be quivering, but if I were in their vicinity I sure would be!); an "intrusion" of cockroaches (you betcha!); a "business" of ferrets; a "tower" of giraffes; a "bloat" of hippopotamuses; a "charm" of hummingbirds; a "mischief" of mice; a "scourge" of mosquitos; a "romp" of otters; an "ostentation" of peacocks; a "prickle" of porcupines; a "scurry" of squirrels; a "chattering" of starlings; a "streak" or "ambush" of tigers; and a "dazzle" of zebras.

And just look at what a bunch of snails is called: an "escargatoire." Now if that fancy name doesn't make a snail feel better, he just isn't paying attention.

As it turns out, a group of scorpions is called a "bed." I sure wouldn't want them in bed with me! And I wonder why a group of emus is called a "mob," while a bunch of gnus is an "impossibility." I wouldn't think that gnus would be more impossible than emus. But since I've never met any of either personally, perhaps I'm not entitled to an opinion.

Creatures that inhabit the seas have some very descriptive names, too. How about a "battery" of barracuda; a "wreck" of sea birds; a "gulp" of cormorants; a "screech" of seagulls; a "fever" of stingrays; a "flamboyance" of flamingos. If you've ever spent any time near the water you know that the terms for cormorants, flamingos and seagulls couldn't be better.

You might enjoy some I haven't categorized: a "flange" of baboons; a "piteousness" of turtle doves (what do you suppose that's about?); a "confusion" of guinea fowl; a "lounge" of lizards; a "pomp" of Pekingese; and a "rhumba" of rattlesnakes. Being a Zumba enthusiast, that last one calls up a plethora of unpleasant images for me!

Last but not least, in the political genre we find: a "parliament" of owls; a "coalition" of cheetahs; and (are you ready for this?) a "stubbornness" of rhinoceroses.

Oh, and before I forget, as of today I counted 16 clergy, with more on the way, I hope. And that can only be a good thing for all of us.

* * *

OLD AND HEALTHY? YES INDEED

An hour or so ago I climbed out of the shower, shivering from the needles of ice (well, not quite, but it felt that way) coming from the showerhead. Why, you may ask, would I be taking an ice cold shower? I asked myself the same question until remembering that I recently spent about an hour, mesmerized, in front of my laptop, listening to an author who wanted to give me the secret to curing diabetes. While he was getting around to the bottom line, with testimonials and so on, I had time to brush my teeth and sort yesterday's mail. Because the time I was investing was growing exponentially I decided to hear him out until the bitter end.

Of course, the first step to the cure was to buy his book which decreased in price as the commercial went on. Since I wasn't about to spend even $39.99 on something written by Mr. Carlyle and the mysterious Dr. Gray, I was about to sign off when I heard the words, "cold shower." Dr. Gray wants us to know that icy showers act to loosen up and flush away the insidious white fat that is a major contributor to diabetes. Well, I had actually heard about white vs. brown fat so decided that daily cold showers were doable. "After all," I thought to myself as I often do, "how bad could it be?" I discovered that icy showers *are* doable, but not any fun, no way, no how!

I managed to endure them, first, because one only has to stay under the cold water for 30 seconds and, second, because I apply the "how to cook a frog" principle. If you want to cook a frog and you throw it into a pot of boiling water, it will jump out of the pot. Instead, you can fool the frog by putting it in a pot of cold water and heating it slowly until, the next thing you know, you have a cooked frog. The same process works, in reverse of course, for icy showers. You should know that I first wrote these words in August. By Thanksgiving I was no longer eager, or even interested, in curing my diabetes with cold showers. It just got way too uncomfortable.

Since that time I had a severe case of bronchitis and learned, quite by accident, that one of the secrets for dealing with diabetes is….EAT LESS, DUMMY! A lot less, actually. I don't know how it works for you, but when I'm really sick I lose my appetite and along with it a couple of pounds, and this leads to lower blood sugar readings. All goes well until I feel better. And we all know what happens next. Making up for lost time (and missed desserts) is not a good idea!

I should mention here that I've always been an enthusiastic eater. These days I call myself a "foodie," a term with a certain cachet to it, no? Back in the day we were just hearty eaters. My mom and my aunts were all good cooks, so I saw no reason to hold back. One of my favorite teenage snacks was two of my mother's homemade Toll House cookies connected Oreo-style with a filling of peanut butter and American cheese! The last person I told that to gagged just thinking about it. In those days I could eat what I wanted and still keep a small waistline …. but there's no point in dwelling on long-past glory.

These days we hear conflicting things about staying healthy, old or not. One week we can benefit immensely from drinking coffee. The next week we hear that it's *bad* to have that third cup. Later, "moderation" is the word. Well, we knew that anyway, didn't we?

The argument that intrigues me the most is how much alcohol is good for the average senior citizen. The latest I've heard is one drink per day for women and two for men. Well, I enjoy a glass of wine, or even better, a scotch and soda, with the best of them, but does this mean I *absolutely must* knock one back every single day? What if it turned out that I was an incipient alcoholic? Who is paying attention to important things like that? Somebody has to! What kind of a government are we running anyway?

So this is my advice for everyone who wants to stay healthy. Listen to your body when it talks to you. But if you don't hear anything, just enjoy your life, and your food, while you can.

* * *

THE JOY OF SOX

Do you remember putting on your first pair of bobby socks? Neither do I, but I do remember the joy of pairing them with saddle shoes and the ubiquitous circle skirt, complete with crinoline. Socks were an important part of a girl's wardrobe back then. That is, one had to have them, but they were a standard item. As far as I remember, it was pretty much one-size, one-style fits all.

My friend Dotty's mother, in her continuing, valiant battle to reconcile her native Swedish tongue with teen girl talk, always insisted we put our socks on with our "gungadins" (dungarees) and huaraches, which she called "cockaroaches," in the belief that cold feet led to many and varied diseases. Dotty's little brother, whom we enjoyed tormenting by hiding his socks, stood in the living room and yelled, "You are a bunch of BASKETS!" As we all grew up, Dotty tried to tease him about the "baskets" word, but since he towered over her at six foot four and didn't have much of a sense of humor, she only tried it once.

As a young mother of two lively little boys, I needed my socks and sneakers most of the time. Everyone in the household wore socks, and they often needed mending. Never mind if your toes got corns from rubbing on the mended part. Throwing them out wasn't an option as long as there were needle and thread available.

But I really hated those socks. They just didn't seem attractive anymore, even though I still needed them. None of my friends wanted to wear socks, either. It was kind of a love-hate relationship. So any time we could get rid of the sneakers, and therefore, the socks, we did. We decided we absolutely needed sandals for the summer, so that we could leave those ugly white socks in the drawer. And the more time we could spend at the beach, the less we would have to worry about sock-lines on our ankles.

When I returned to the business world, socks just about vanished from my consciousness. It was high heels and pantyhose. Socks were not only gauche, but impossible under the circumstances. You understand that this was before everyone ran around wearing sneakers with their business clothes. And I liked running around the house barefoot when I got home. Outdoors, the grass felt good on bare feet, and no one had yet heard of Lyme disease.

The years went by, and I must confess, I rarely had a second thought relative to socks. But one day, somewhat older and less concerned about whether or not my legs looked good, I decided that sox were really great. I found that they had other uses besides keeping my feet warm.

The very best thing about them has been how helpful they are when I travel by air. How healthy it feels, when I have to take off my shoes and put them in the airline bin during the security check, to know that my feet do not have to touch the crummy-looking carpet or the dirty floor! All because of those cute sox.

Now that I've reached my dotage, I'm allowed to keep my shoes on when traveling by air. But I can wear the cute sox anyway.

Now I have come to love and cherish my sox. I have some good, heavy ones for the winter, and some with little snowmen and holly leaves and pumpkins for the holidays. Some of them roll all the way up to my knees, and one pair has pink roses all over them. I have some little ones that just come to the tops of my sneakers….in ice cream colors, with polka dots, or stripes. My favorite pair reminds me of the Rainbow Coalition flag.

I don't mend my sox anymore when they wear a hole through the toe. I have reached the point of affluence where I can buy another pair if I want to. Now my sock drawer is stuffed, and hardly any of them are white.

* * *

LANGUAGES AND ACCENTS

Pennsylvanians have told me, often with surprise, that I don't "tawk like a Neh Yawka," even though I was born and raised in Brooklyn and lived most of my life on Long Island. This got me thinking about language and accents that I've heard and come to love over the years.

My first encounter with the idea that my own speech pattern might seem odd was in first or second grade, when the New York City public schools taught music appreciation early on. We were learning about the orchestra, which I pronounced "ork e stra." All these years later I still cringe remembering the laughter from teacher and students alike. When I went home and told my mother, she told me to call my older cousin who could tell me what was wrong, as this sounded just fine to her. I discovered that I had been pronouncing the word with a Swedish accent.

Both my parents had Swedish accents, though my mother's was less obvious that my father's. In Swedish, "v's" and "w's" come out differently that they do in English, and I fondly recall my father coming home from work and remarking that it was "wery vindy" outside.

When I went to work in a Manhattan advertising agency at age 18 I became conscious that co-workers from Staten Island sounded different than those from The Bronx, for example, and I decided that I wanted to sound area-neutral, which I thought would be more chic and sophisticated. I began to think I was getting it right when, on a train to Boston, my seatmate said, "Where do you come from? I don't hear an accent."

Accents were fun, I realized, when I vacationed for a week on Nantucket. By the time my fellow traveler, Shirley, and I headed home, I had inadvertently broadened my "a's" to the point where I might have been taken for an Islander. Shirley thought I was showing off, but it really did come naturally.

A similar situation occurred while I was spending winters in Florida. I often caught myself sporting a pseudo-Southern accent in the company of native Southerners. It was embarrassing, and I learned to be more mindful of what I wanted to say before I said it.

Again, spending five weeks with relatives in Sweden, I adopted some kind of crazy American-accented, English-speaking-Swede style of conversing. At that point, I tried to get myself to think and speak in Swedish. The sentences came out in what I called "baby Swedish," but I persevered, and my relatives appreciated the effort. With one cousin's husband, who had no English at all, I was reduced to drawing pictures on napkins, but somehow we managed until one of their kids showed up to take over the translation.

My aunts and uncles also adopted English when our families got together for holidays. Of course, there was some Swedish conversation, but they thought my cousins and I had forgotten that language. My uncle had a favorite joke which he told whenever he had had a few too many boilermakers. It was a shade off-color (though nothing like what we hear these days), and the grownups were always shocked when we kids sniggered at the punch line, "and that's where the painter put his hand." Don't ask what the rest of the joke was. We've discussed it as adults and no one remembers anything but the punch line.

I took four years of Latin in high school, and while it was an excellent aid for proficiency in English, it really didn't have a special rhythm. Two years of Spanish was more fun, though our teacher taught Castilian style and we were all tongue-tied with the lispy esses. Aside from a love for the sound of the language, all I can remember is how to sing a Christmas carol, *Pastores a Belen* in the Castilian style.

In the one semester I spent at Brooklyn College in 1952, I took a German class. Only one phrase remains with me…. *Du hast ein Vogel*, which our teacher said means "You are crazy," but literally, "You have a bird," presumably flitting around in your noggin. Now I've begun thinking about studying French. I have an audio disc to use in the car, but it's too hard to concentrate on pronunciation while driving.

Over the years I've come to delight in accents and stray words in foreign languages. My very favorite word is *porte-cochere* which is tremendous fun to say, but one rarely has the opportunity to use it in everyday conversation.

Now that I live at Lutherburgh I'm learning some Pennsylvania Dutch words. So far, my favorite is *rutch*, which I've probably spelled incorrectly. I am also quite fond of *kerfuffle*. Not to mention "shoo fly pie" and "funny cake."

So talk to me in other languages, please. I may not understand what you're saying but you will absolutely make my day!

* * *

SMOKING

Once upon a time nicotine was king. It came in many permutations: snuff, chewing tobacco, cigars, cigarettes .... and now it even comes in patches! My father's choice was pipe tobacco. I think it was called Old Overholding, but my mother and I called it Old Overshoes. It smelled B. A. D., and in our little four-room apartment, there was no room for BAD. While Papa was at work, we would open all the windows, even in the dead of winter, to try to air out the smell.

My first boyfriend wouldn't come into the house when my dad was at home. He would sit on the steps outside our apartment door and wait patiently while I put my coat on. Not every boy I went out with was that fastidious, and one even boldly asked my father if he could try his pipe. My father laughed and handed it over, and Frank almost didn't make it to the bathroom.

When I was fifteen, I decided it was time to try smoking for myself. I knew my parents would be outraged if they found out, but I was willing to try getting away with it by chewing lots of gum, all the time. I smoked my first Lucky Strike at Dotty's house. Her mother smoked, and so did Dotty, so it seemed logical to take my first deep drag there. Now it was my turn to end up in the bathroom, coughing and choking, much to the amusement of both Dotty and her mom. But she was a kind of hands-off mother, and she never did tell my parents.

Smoking cigarettes was the height of sophistication my friends and I thought. After all, didn't Barbara Stanwyck always have a glass of champagne in one hand and a cigarette in the other? Didn't The Continental (do you remember him?) have one as he lounged against the fireplace, looking incredibly *foreign* and sexy. The French accent didn't hurt, either. And for those of us in the girl's high school, who were thought of in some circles as "grinds," cigarettes were the perfect way of showing that we were NOT grinds, but ordinary, down-and-dirty women.

Years of smoking cigarettes caught up with me when I was about 40 years old. I discovered that my feet were falling asleep at strange times and decided that my circulation must be in jeopardy. I suddenly remembered my father-in-law's term for cigarettes: coffin nails. Maybe it was time to quit for good. Previous resolutions to restore my lungs to health had usually meant a week or two of deprivation and then a run to the grocery store for a fresh pack.

In desperation I went to the tobacco shop and bought some cigars. Normally, cigars were quite appealing to me. On holidays, which my parents and I spent with aunts, uncles, and cousins, the after-dinner male ritual was: good cigars, boilermakers, and pinochle. So the smell of cigars held good memories of happy family times. But somehow I knew that cigars, delightful though they were, would be my liberation from tobacco forever!

I found some very large, bluish-black stogies at about ten cents each, and bought five of them. The label said they were blueberry flavored, which at the time I considered a plus. I decided not to try this at home, since I didn't want the kids to know what I was doing. They had seen me fail before, and I didn't think it was good for their psychological development to see this once again. And my husband was still smoking, so there would be no sympathy from that quarter.

I was working part-time as a receptionist at a small, local advertising agency. Everyone there smoked, so I felt sure that no one would notice the cigars. On Monday morning I lit up and was immediately enveloped in a miasma of foul-smelling, smoky clouds. It was disgusting, but I knew immediately that this was going to work. The smell was so bad it made my eyes water; my mouth tasted like a sewer. I was really afraid to inhale, and I rapidly discovered that there were absolutely no rewards involved in smoking anymore. By noontime, my boss came out of his office and said, "I appreciate what you're trying to do, but do you think you'll be finished sometime soon?"

For the next year or two I kept a pack of cigarettes in the freezer, just in case. After a while they became a fixture there, like the little packs of gel you freeze to keep your lunches cold. I'd like to say I never missed my cigarettes again, but that would be a lie. For almost a year I had to give up coffee, too, because a cup of joe just wasn't the same without a cigarette.

And let's not discuss cocktails. Minus the cigarettes they may just be a headache.

* * *

Dad at Work with Ever-Present Pipe

Mom and Dad (With Pipe)

OH, THOSE CLOTHES!

Women, do you remember the gorgeous clothes we wore back in the '50s? Looking at the way people dress today, it certainly is a different style.

Formality has gone out the window in favor of comfort. I can relate to that, especially now that fancy shoes make my feet swell after an hour or so of wear, and slim waistlines are a thing of the long-ago past.

My three girl cousins were all older than I, and my sense of style was frequently inspired by what they wore. When I was 14 my mother promised me I, too, could start wearing more mature styles, and I could hardly contain myself the day we went downtown to pick out my first girdle. The mind absolutely boggles! By the time the '60s rolled around I couldn't wait to throw my girdles away!

I'm not sure when dungarees became popular, but I wore them in my mid-teens, though going to school, or to church (God forbid!) in any kind of pants was unheard of.

Skirts were the thing, with the ubiquitous bobby socks and saddle shoes for school and casual wear.

Girlfriends in Everyday Clothes

My favorite item of clothing was my frilly crinoline. I only had one, so I had to take really good care of it. It was for wear with party-type dresses to puff out the full skirts. Under the crinoline were the nylon stockings (no panty hose back then) with seams up the back. These were secured either by that girdle or by a garter belt, and getting those seams straight took a lot of time if you didn't want to put a run in them. Looking at old pictures I'm amazed that any of us thought a girdle was necessary. Now would be the time, but trust me, it will never happen!

When we went into Manhattan to work every morning we looked fresh and put-together in our beautiful business suits, with hats and gloves and high-heeled shoes. I fondly remember my two seersucker suits, one pink and one blue, ideal for summer wear. The subway ride was long …. at least an hour, depending on connections …. but it wasn't much of a problem in the cooler weather.

Summer was another thing entirely. No such thing as an air conditioned train, and by late afternoon, when heat had been storing up all day in the tunnels, the put-together look had disappeared forever.

Hot in our jackets and hats, gloves tucked away in purses, feet throbbing in those high heels, we stood on those steaming platforms just hoping our train would be on time. Except for Katie.

Even in the most humid weather at five-thirty in the afternoon, she looked as though she had just emerged from her boudoir in perfect array. All summer long Katie was the object of envy and occasional hatred, depending on the temperature.

If our work clothes were pretty and stylish, our party dresses were even better! Beautiful fabrics, darts in the bodices ("What is a dart?" some will ask.) Little buttons up the back. Discreet cleavage. Very, very nice.

Big skirts with crinolines beneath, or slender sheaths that emphasized what friend Dotty called our "Swedish childbearing hips." Sometimes I dream about those clothes.

Party Clothes

When I moved to Ed's house I packed up a load of outfits that had been stashed in a closet in the vain hope that someday I would be able to wear them again. I donated them to a local theatrical group and they were very excited to have my "Jackie Kennedy" style pink suit but were disappointed that I hadn't saved my pillbox hat with the little veil.

These days I almost never wear dresses, and I don't own a suit any more. I donated all my work clothes to Dress for Success at one of our semi-annual church women's events. But even if I had kept them, they wouldn't fit.

That's why I keep old photos.

* * *

WHO'S KEEPING TIME

"Keeping time" is an interesting phrase, especially because time is clearly not something capable of being kept. No matter what we do, time, like Old Man River, just keeps rollin' along.

It makes me very happy that no two clocks in my apartment tell the same time. One of my clocks, in fact, doesn't keep any time at all, but I do intend to have that one fixed eventually. Well, technically, it is 22 minutes to eight twice a day, so I suppose that clock *is* keeping time after all.

I love that I only keep time "more or less" these days. I think it's a great analogy for being retired. After all, unless we want to count medical appointments, entertainment, religious services and Lutherburgh committee meetings, where do we have to be at a set time anymore? Can't we just loll around, doing the crossword puzzle and sudoku, taking naps, checking out what's on the movie channel and strolling down to the dining room hoping we can get a seat even though we forgot to make a reservation?

On one hand this seems like a pretty comfortable way of life, but after a few days of basking on the balcony with a good book and playing computer games in the hope of sharpening my slowly-turning-to-mush brain, the idea of time being wasted begins to penetrate my consciousness and, like Peggy Lee, I start to contemplate the question, "Is That All There Is?"

Well, it doesn't have to be. One of the things I've noticed since I've gotten this old is that in some ways I feel a lot like the person I was at age 18. I liked who I was back then, even though I was very aware of a number of flaws of both appearance and character. That person disappeared during my 20s with the pressures of adulthood. I think she has returned now because I am leading a relatively carefree life, a lot like the one I led in my teens.

Age 18

Anyway, being a teenager again, at least in spirit, has given me the guts to try some things I didn't try years ago due to being self-conscious, or scared, or unable to spare the money required. For instance, I wanted to take lessons as a kid. I didn't care what kind of lessons that might be, but I would have preferred dance. My parents never told me why I couldn't have lessons, but I suspect that it had to do with finances. So now I'm taking tap here at Lutherburgh, and even though I'm really bad at it, I'm having fun. Sadly, the old brain isn't connecting with the old feet, so I'm thinking one step and doing something else. But I sure love the sound of those taps!

Tappy Feet

It's the 18-year-old who has given me the impetus to write a book. I've been writing on and off since about fourth grade and part of the appeal has always been to amuse other people with my ideas. Back then I would write little stories and read them to my classmates at recess. I have no memory of the plots of these efforts, but I do remember that one of my early heroes was named Aubrey Murdock. Go figure.

But when I started thinking seriously about a book I thought, as I often do, "How hard could it be? Go for it." So that's what I've done.

The young Helen has also led me to take up the boomba in my mature years which in itself isn't such a big deal, but standing up in front of my peers and letting them watch me do it, is.

If I have the time next year and if it's still available, I think I'd like to take advantage of the Lutherburgh offer to learn how to play the cello. I've always liked the sound of it, but my inability to read music has deterred me.

I really should ask my grandson about this. When he was about ten he decided to take cello in school. Why? Because he could sit down while he played.

Grandson with Cello

I've heard a lot of people remark that time passes so much more quickly now than it did when we were children. I frankly don't know how it is that I am now 80 years old, but it does have one big advantage: the ability to play "the old lady card." If the grocery bags are just a little too heavy to manage, I can often find someone to help by mentioning my age. This also works well when I need to ask for some special consideration, or must explain why I just can't do "this" or donate to "that."

Time passes, and eventually, so will I. I want to use the time I've got left to catch up on all the things I haven't gotten around to yet.

How about you?

* * *

COFFEE

On the TV news today I saw a feature about people putting butter in their coffee to facilitate weight loss. "Wow," I thought, "what a way to get skinny! It would allow me to indulge in two of my vices and incur a benefit at the same time. How good is that?"

Second thoughts brought me back to reality, since I can't honestly believe that a daily dose of butter could possibly help with weight loss. Olive oil, maybe, but how would that taste in coffee? Against my principles of trying almost anything once, I decided that buttered coffee was just too much to swallow. However, it did cause me to meditate on coffee and my love of it all these many years.

My personal history with coffee goes back a veeery long way. It's hard to believe, but I had my first cup at about age four. My memory is fuzzy as to how much of it I actually drank. It must have been laced with lots of milk and sugar, but it was my father's way of getting to enjoy his own Sunday morning cup of joe.

It was his custom to get up early in the morning and walk down to the Norwegian bakery a few blocks away, where he would carefully choose fancy buns and cookies for our Sunday treat. When he got home he would put on the coffee pot and prepare a tray which he served to my mother and me in their bed. Since he never, ever, did any other kind of "housework" this was an exciting event indeed, and it never got old. It was my habit to dunk the buns and cookies into my father's coffee cup, until the day he implored my mother, "Please! Give her her own cup," pointing to the sludge that covered the inside of his. And the rest, as they say, is history.

So when I realized recently that my love for coffee had diminished somewhat, it was cause for concern. Seventy-five years had passed with only one hiatus being the time when I gave up smoking and couldn't even think of having coffee without a cigarette to go with it. That period of deprivation lasted a year, and by then the cigarette urge had left me, but the call of the coffee pot had not.

So as I was drinking tea for breakfast the other morning, I understood that this was a potential identity crisis. Am I not a first generation Swedish-American? My ancestors did not pass a day without their coffee. My cousins who reside there drink *kaffe* numerous times daily: first thing in the morning; for breakfast; around 11 a.m. and again at 3 p.m.; with lunch; usually for dinner and always after; when someone comes to visit; when visiting friends; during business meetings; from a thermos (with buns and cookies) when traveling, by car or public transportation; at cafes during the long twilight of summer evenings in the far north; at every party on any occasion. Who might I be if I gave up coffee for good?

In my teens, after Confirmation Class and Luther League meetings, anywhere from five to 30 of the youth of Salem Lutheran Church would descend upon Andersen's Ice Cream Parlor and consume gallons of coffee. It was a lot cheaper than ice cream. There was a booth in the back that would accommodate ten comfortably, and another six or eight if we smooshed ourselves together, and we were really annoyed when the gang from Epiphany got there ahead of us.

If we had the money for ice cream we would wait until some of the guys were able to borrow cars and then drive to Jahn's in Queens, famous all over the city for its specialty, The Kitchen Sink. Normally it took at least four of us to finish one, but Tiny Lundqvist packed one in all by himself one night, to raucous cheers from the gang.

After starting work in Manhattan in a corporate typing pool I couldn't wait for coffee breaks. Not only did I need the fix, but spending my days behind one in a long line of manual typewriters clicking and clanging away was messing with my head. When I was promoted to private secretary coffee became my reward for braving the subway ride an hour each way from Brooklyn to Broad Street.

Visiting New Orleans during the World's Fair I turned on to their dark, bitter, flavorful brew. For a while I sent away for Gevalia, knowing that since it was a Swedish brand it had to be good. When I first moved to Pennsylvania I went crazy with the local market's special blends until it began to seem irresponsible to spend that kind of money on something that would ultimately be flushed away.

For years coffee has been my drink-of-choice, my motivator, my companion (in lieu of a dog), my comfort food (followed by homemade macaroni and cheese), my cheerer-upper, and as reliable as a best friend. Now that I'm old and diabetic, I can't rely on alcohol (especially for breakfast), and macaroni and cheese is pretty much off the menu, so I guess I will have to keep the coffee coming for a while longer, whether I crave it or not.

Time for Coffee

* * *

DO YOU SPEAK ENGLISH?

In June, 2001, I traveled for the first (and so far, only) time to Sweden to visit the country of my ancestors and, perhaps, meet the present members of my mother's and father's families. My cousin Katrin, who had helped me plan the five week trip, had informed me that she had contacted "everyone" of our cousins and I shouldn't be disappointed if I met only a few of them. There was no interest, she explained, in a family reunion.

I decided not to take it personally, because my mother had told me that in the old days many poor Swedes who had done well in America were prone to return "home" wearing furs, flashing cash, and generally acting obnoxious. Swedes have long memories, so I couldn't blame them for whatever they might have been thinking about me, even though we had never met. Well, once I got there I acted like a decent human being, even cooking up a dish of eggplant parmigiana for a *Midsomer* Day dinner, and that changed things.

 Another cousin, Anna, had been my pen pal when we were 10 years old, she writing in Swedish and me replying in English. It was hard for her to find someone to translate, since her family lived in the country and our generation hadn't received instruction in English except in the big cities, so our connection didn't last long. But she decided it was time for us to meet, and her sister Inga, with husband Ben, invited a large number of the family to a barbeque.

The problem was that, although Anna spoke English quite well, she was embarrassed to do so. She was determined to speak it perfectly, or not at all. I had stopped speaking Swedish when I started kindergarten, so my Swedish language skills left a lot to be desired. *No one else*, including her husband, had any English whatsoever, so it was decided that their old friend, Gust Olsson, would be invited along to act as interpreter. Gust wisely spent his winters in New Orleans, returning to his home in Vanersborg only for the glorious summers in the Swedish countryside.

It was about an hour's drive to Inga and Ben's home. When we arrived at the party there were assembled about 25 cousins, some with spouses, somewhat wary, but ready to enjoy the reunion that no one had wanted to have.

As it happened, this party was taking place on July 4th. I knew it was good Swedish etiquette to bring presents to one's hosts, and since I had no idea how many people I might encounter during my visit, among the gifts I had brought were a package of about 50 inexpensive American flag tack pins. They might as well have been made of gold for all the pleasure they provided. My cousins pinned on the flags and declared themselves Americans for the day!

I had brought along my parents' old photo album, filled with pictures of people I didn't know, pasted to crumbling black pages by means of four little white paper corners, and this caused a huge sensation! Here were pictures of family members who had immigrated and never returned, as well as some who had decided that America was not so much and opted to return home to Sweden. Here were photos of my cousins when they were children, sent with loving letters so necessary to assuage the homesickness, as well as photos of the children born in the New World.

As the day progressed, with lots of hospitality, including unlimited bottles of beer, folks started to loosen up a bit. By the time dinner was ready, Anna was saying to Gust "tell Helen….." and going on in perfectly good English for a paragraph or two or three. Gust, who had enjoyed the unlimited beer along with all the rest of us, would very seriously take my hand and repeat the whole thing …. in Swedish! By the time we were ready to go home, I was speaking Swedish (unfortunately like a four-year-old), and Gust was asking for my phone number in English and in Swedish.

This was only one of many interesting days I spent examining my roots, and I would suggest to everyone, wherever your family came from, go there and just get the feeling of the country and its people. It can be a life-changing experience.

* * *

OUT, OUT, FOUL TONSILS!

Some people never have to give a thought to their tonsils. Others have had them removed when they were little kids, and others have had this surgery as adults. I've had my tonsils out twice, which is probably not a record, but may be a little bit unusual.

The first time I was about five years old and don't remember a thing. The second time I was 28, and it was all because my sons, Steven and David, had been sick just about every weekend all winter, first one and then the other, and our doctor decided that their tonsils had to go. But first, he said, I ought to have my tonsils out, since I had probably been infecting the kids all along.

Adult tonsillectomies were same-day procedures, and I do remember something about that. I was given a hospital gown on top of my clothes and something *delightful* was shot into my arm. I knew what was going on, but I didn't give a hoot. I walked, assisted by a large male nurse, into the operating room where I was seated on a bar stool with my head against a big pillow that was taped to the wall behind me.

"Open up," the doctor said, and the next thing I knew the offending body parts were gone. "I want to see them," I told the O. R. nurse, who looked horrified. "Well, let her!" the doctor replied. I only wish I could remember what they looked like! All that has stayed in my mind is a mason jar with liquid and something else in it. This would be a lot better story if I still had that memory.

About a month later, the boys were booked into the same hospital for their tonsillectomies. We tried to explain ahead of time what was going to happen. Steve was about five, and he seemed to get the idea to some degree, but David, at two and a half, wasn't ready for either the explanation or the surgery. However, they were both really happy to see their Grandma who came out to Deer Park from Brooklyn to go with us. She worried a lot, so it was easier to bring her along than to report on what was happening by phone.

We saw the boys "settled" in twin cribs, low to the floor with high sides. When the nurse insisted we leave the room, both of them stood there like little prisoners, holding onto the bars and wailing. It broke my heart, and my mother looked as though she might collapse.

As we expected when we finally got our wits together, the surgery went well, and we were instructed to pick up the children the next morning. When we arrived, Steven had a welcoming smile on his face, but David's was a storm cloud! He was *not* happy, and he was *not* forgiving. My mom and I had become The Enemy.

Steven was easily mollified with the promise of all the ice cream he could eat to soothe his sore throat. David didn't want ice cream. At home, we restored David to his crib in hopes he might relax a bit, but he wasn't having any kind of comfort from us.

Both boys loved my mom's pancakes and we were pretty sure David's heart would melt when he got a whiff of them cooking.

I got his favorite book of the moment, "Danny's Pancakes," sat in the rocking chair next to his crib and started reading, but that didn't help either. I tried to lift him from the crib onto my lap, but he made himself stiff as a board and he wouldn't say a word.

David wasn't very verbal until he was about three years old, and it was clear that he wasn't speaking to us now!

Steven, on the other hand, had rambled on enthusiastically whenever someone would listen, even if we couldn't always understand him, from the time he was about ten months old.

David didn't have to talk, because Steven seemed to intuit what he needed and was happy to keep us posted. "He's mad at you," Steven informed me. Well, I had figured that out on my own. David finally succumbed to the lure of pancakes (with ice cream) when he got hungry enough, and healing proceeded normally after that.

Happiness is No Tonsils!

Just in case David ever reads this, I think I need to mention that when he did decide to speak for himself, he talked in full sentences and with relatively good grammar. I guess he didn't want to do it until he could do it well, which has pretty much been his way of operating ever since.

So now everyone's tonsils are out, and we rarely get sore throats any more…..thank goodness.

* * *

MUSIC

A few hours ago I returned from a Bach concert performed at an enormous Lutheran church downtown. Listening to the Fifth Brandenburg Concerto in this magnificent setting made me say a prayer of thanksgiving for all the music in which I've become immersed since moving to Lutherburgh.

Although I've always enjoyed music I never had a chance to get so involved with it before. In the 1940s the New York City public school system provided music education for children in the lower grades, and we were taught little ditties to sing which were supposed to help us remember the names of composers and compositions. Until recently I could remember many of them, but right now all that comes to mind is "*Rustles of Spring* b-uh-y Sinding."

I do remember in second grade I was told not to sing when our little school chorus stood up to perform. That scarred me for life and the one thing I absolutely won't do in public is sing. Of course, church services are something else again, and I take literally the words of the psalmist, "O make a joyful noise unto the Lord." If noise is okay with the Lord, I'm happy to oblige.

As a teenager I enjoyed the popular music of our time, especially because we were often dancing to it. Jazz was a special favorite, and when the man I eventually married took me on our first date to a jazz club in lower Manhattan, I was really impressed.

Central Terrace was located on an upper floor in a loft building which was reached by boarding a big, commercial elevator. As the elevator ascended the music got louder, until the doors opened and we were hit with a blast of sound that took my breath away. This was my first experience visiting a club, and I was underage; no one seemed to care and we sure had a good time! This first date started us on a path that led to our wedding song being "When the Saints Go Marching In." This was at the reception, of course; neither of us had the nerve to ask Pastor Hanson to let us walk up the aisle to that tune!

The Saints Go Marching Out
Of Church

When my husband and I got married and had children we decided we ought to become more serious about our musical preferences. I suspect this was my husband's way of getting the fancy stereo equipment he wanted, and I can see him in my mind's eye sitting on the curb across the street from our house with the volume turned all the way up, listening to "Romeo and Juliet," with woofers and tweeters (whatever they are) going full blast.

That was our one big venture into the classics. We were both more comfortable with Barbra Streisand and *La Bamba* than with Beethoven. But after my divorce I found that I couldn't listen to our old favorites without turning into mush, so I made an effort to listen to radio stations that offered classical music and soon became a big fan of New York's favorite classical music station.

For two seasons my friend Linny and I had tickets to the New York Philharmonic, sitting just one row down from the back wall of the very top balcony of the theater. We were so far up that getting to our seats was scary. Once we were seated, however, we really enjoyed the experience.

Once in a while tickets to the Long Island Philharmonic became available through the nonprofit agency where I worked. After we had given them to our clients, staff were allowed to use any that were left over. I heard some wonderful music then, but if the tickets weren't *gratis* I rarely went.

A favorite way to get a good dose of the classics was at the Philharmonic's summertime concerts in the park. The park was located near the Great South Bay, and while the ride in was fine it often took an hour or more to get out when the concert was over …. so many cars leaving at the same time!

We would fill up the cars with music-lovers and fill the trunks with snacks and drinks, beach chairs and blankets, and head out early in order to get a good spot in front of the band shell. One year the fog coming off the bay got so thick that the concert came to a premature end. The conductor explained that the strings were absorbing the dampness and couldn't stay tuned properly.

From time to time over the years I've had the urge to learn to play an instrument. The problem is, I haven't had the will to commit to learning how to read music so I can begin to learn the instrument. I partially solved that problem back in the '60s when I talked my husband into giving me a little chord organ for Christmas. I installed it in a corner of the dining room, bought some play-by-the-numbers sheet music, and had a ball with it, especially around the Christmas holidays.

Later, when I was single, friends would come over and we would sing carols while I played the chord organ, still reading the numbers. Hey, no one had a piano. This was the closest thing we could get to an evening salon with music and *glogg*, a Swedish Christmas drink which deserves a story all its own.

When I moved to Ed's house the chord organ moved to the upstairs bedroom. It was a very big room and the organ didn't get in our way. When I felt like playing it, still reading the numbers, I didn't drown out the TV in the living room downstairs.

I enjoyed that organ for many years, but I knew I couldn't take it to Lutherburgh. There was just no place to put it in my small apartment. So I gave it to a little boy who loved it so much that he would beg his mother to visit me so he could get a crack at it. Talk about making someone happy!

Now here I am living in the Lehigh Valley, and I've heard more good music in the past few years than I did in my whole life before, especially when the great Allentown Band sets up at the front entrance of Lutherburgh and we hear the best outdoor concert ever!

I'm looking forward to lots more good music for as long as I'm able to hear it.

* * *

DON'T FALL DOWN

Everywhere you go at Lutherburgh you know that the words of wisdom we live by are "Don't fall down!" From a fall comes all kinds of misery and grief, and we do not need this in our old age.

Up to this point I've never broken any bones, ever. This is kind of surprising, since I was quite active as a child, especially roller skating hour after hour downhill on 56th Street in Brooklyn. Roller skates were metal, screwed onto the bottom of one's shoes with a skate key and strapped across the instep. Occasionally they fell off on the way down. I wasn't the only one to take regular flops, but I was the only one not to break a bone. Skinned knees were a regular occurrence, but we had lots of band-aids at home so that wasn't a big deal.

I didn't hurt any bones until after I was divorced and living alone in the family home. My kitchen dishwasher was at the end of the counter just around the corner from the hallway, and late one night I got up for something or other, walked down the hall in the dark, and slammed my left shin into the side of the dishwasher which I had left open to aid in the drying process.

Wow! Did that smart! I jumped up and down for a while on the other foot, but that didn't help much. So I took two aspirins and went back to bed, my leg aching badly, planning to see my doctor in the morning.

When I climbed out of bed at 6 a.m., oh my. My leg looked as though there was a football under the skin over my shinbone. I touched it gingerly and my finger sank into the skin in a way that scared me speechless. I never did see the doctor because he told me what to do over the phone. That was 30 years ago or so, but to this day my shin bone hurts when the weather gets damp.

While I was living at Ed's house I had a bad fall on our blacktop driveway. My car was parked there overnight during a freezing rainstorm, and in the morning it looked clear and safe. But this was my first encounter with black ice, and when I went to open the car door I slipped on the ice and went down on my right side. By all rights I should have broken my hip; I didn't. But for the next few days it felt like my whole skeleton was in the wrong place. Or perhaps it was in the alternate universe. Wherever or whatever, it felt weird.

While I was living in the house next door to my church, I went up my front steps, tripped over my own feet, and smashed against the wrought iron railing. My glasses wound up sideways on my face and I had cuts on my nose and cheek, but the glasses didn't even break! They looked really peculiar, though, with the stems bent out of shape. When I put them on I looked like a deranged Lucille Ball in one of her nutty TV episodes.

One weekend we had a spectacular snowstorm, and since I lived right next to the church I decided I should go there just in case someone actually showed up for services. The pastor, living more than a mile away, decided to cancel services that morning, a first in the history of our congregation. He would have had a lot of trouble getting there, and the newscasters were telling everyone not to go out unless it was *really* necessary.

Well, I struggled out my side door and down to the sidewalk, where a narrow path had been shoveled by one of the parishioners some time earlier. It was a relatively short walk, and I managed to slog up to the door of the office wing and let myself in. Three people showed up for church. All of them lived within a few blocks and all of them had walked there. Well, we decided to have a bible study and sing a few hymns and the tiny congregation left for home reasonably well-satisfied.

One Big Snowbank in Front of the House

When I left the building to walk back home the avenue had been cleared a bit, and a few dopey drivers were barreling down the street. Someone veered toward me, I jumped back and wound up neck deep in a snow bank, falling in rear end first. Have you ever fallen into a large bank of soft snow? I was thinking I might have to stay there until spring. All my flailing around didn't do a bit of good; there was no way to get a purchase from which to propel myself up and out. Then I saw a man exiting the deli across the street. I yelled for help; he crossed the street and dragged me out of the snow bank. No broken bones then, either, though it would have been pretty hard to break anything under the circumstances. The most damage done was to my dignity!

The last fall I took was in 2010 when I decided I needed Chinese food for lunch and walked over to the shopping center across the street from the church. I was moving at a good pace when I hit a patch of black ice. My feet slid out in front of me and I slammed down on my rear end. That hurt!

A small white box truck stopped right there and a pleasant young man stepped out. "Are you hurt, ma'am?" he asked.

Don't you love that you become "ma'am" when you start getting wrinkled? I said no and he offered to help me up. "Well, if you don't I'm going to have to sit here until the ice melts." Might as well be gracious, I thought.

The nice young man got some traction and dragged me up off the ice. "Are you sure you aren't hurt?"

"I'm sure," I replied. "Oh, good," he said. "Now I can laugh. You sure looked funny going down."

So far I've managed to stay upright here at Lutherburgh. I did need to use a cane for a little while when my left knee went out on me for a few days. (I forgot to mention a fall I had when taking my boys ice skating on the lake in 1965. That one gave me a really fat knee and occasionally comes back to haunt me.) The only problem about the sore knee was that I had to miss my Zumba fitness classes for a few weeks.

I try to be mindful when I'm out and about, and even in my apartment. I'm sure you are taking as good care of yourself as I'm trying to do.

Keep up the good work.

* * *

"Let's Go to the Beach, Mom"
Author, Age 5

GOING TO THE BEACH

Coming from Long Island via Brooklyn as I did, I've always felt a special affinity for the ocean. Recently I had been walking around Luther Crest telling everyone that I was missing the beach, when a friend took pity on me and invited me to go with her "down the Shore" for a long weekend. It was chilly, and it was windy, and it was wonderful!

With all of this joy related to water (and I'm a Pisces, too) you would think I would be a swimmer, but not at all. Family lore has it that when I was about four years old and we were on vacation at Asbury Park, my father insisted on taking me into the waves and dunking me up and down. Evidently I didn't like that treatment, and I was a teenager before I would venture of my own volition beyond the edge of the incoming tide.

But the beach was another story. Sand and sun were never scary, and never disappointing. When I got to be about seven or eight and we were living in Bay Ridge, Brooklyn, my mother would pack a lunch, gather up an old blanket, I would run to get my pail and shovel, and we would take the subway to Coney Island. I think it took about a half-hour, and the anticipation was exquisite. The train would come up from the tunnel into sunlight about half-way there, and I would bounce up and down all the way to the last stop.

Before we could actually get on the beach we would have to walk past the roller coaster, always filled with screaming people as it rumbled its way up the long track that led to bedlam. When we reached the boardwalk, there was the heart-stopping aroma of Nathan's Hot Dogs, and the machine that pumped out clumps of noxious-pink, sugary cotton candy. If by chance mom had not brought our lunch along (which was a rarity and a wonderful treat) we would have both of these delicacies on our way to finding the perfect spot near the water to set up our blanket.

These simple outings gave way to teenage beach parties when I joined the "crowd" of Confirmation class graduates and Junior Fellowship Leaguers. All summer we went around in packs of as many as 25 boys and girls, almost joined at the hip. Sometimes someone borrowed a car. Other times we anted up the 10 cents for subway fare, and sometimes we went down to the Belt Parkway in groups of three or four and hitchhiked our way to the beach. Of course, our parents had no idea we were transporting ourselves that way, or we would have been grounded at once, and possibly forever.

As newlyweds in a Brooklyn apartment my husband and I would often drive out on the Belt Parkway to Plum Beach. Swimming wasn't allowed, but the beach was fine for walking, and there was a quiet parking lot for folks who were inclined in that direction. Even after Steven was born we would ride out on a Sunday afternoon. When he was an infant we could put him in the car bed (no one has these anymore) and know he would pass out from the motion of the car. When he got a little older Steve would like to play in the sand while we enjoyed the breezes off the bay.

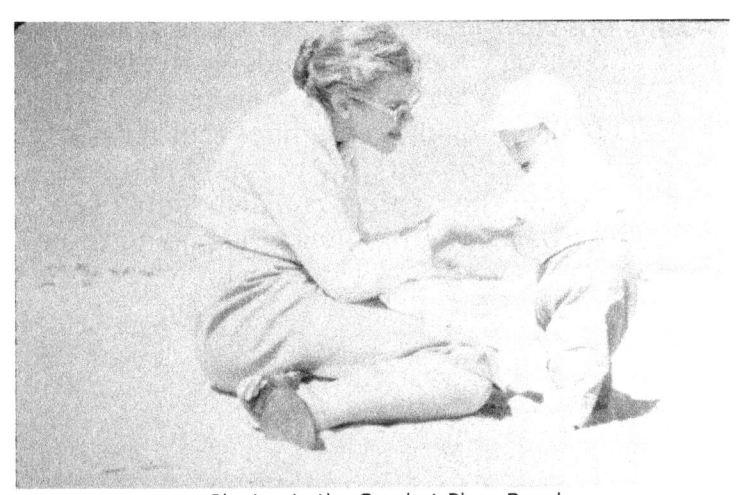

Playing in the Sand at Plum Beach

Timed passed and when Steven was about two and a half years old we moved to Long Island. Just about that time a lovely bridge had been built that allowed for travel from the mainland to the barrier beaches which were about 20 minutes away by car. Prior to that, only folks who had access to a boat could get there. My friends and I would take the kids (by this time we had added David to our little clan) and spend hours talking and tanning while the kids knocked themselves out running the beach. Everyone slept well on summer nights.

For a number of years in the middle part of my life I almost never went to the beach. Between the kids and their events, my part-time jobs and church responsibilities, there rarely seemed to be time. But when things started to get problematic at home, I rediscovered the beach. The boys were grown up and didn't need me for much, and I spent most of my Saturday afternoons roaming the water's edge, thinking and trying to figure out where my life was heading. While I was in the process of divorce I was in a serious depression, but the sea breezes and ocean smells had a beneficial effect. I vividly remember that for many months everything looked grey to me. Then one day while walking the beach I could suddenly see color again! That's when I knew I was going to be all right.

Beach at Fire Island

Years later, after the death of my dear partner, Ed, I spent day after day at the beach, camera in hand. I was retired by then so there was nothing to keep me away. It was healing, and I'm so grateful for that. The beach had been a special place for us, especially in the winter when it's peaceful, uncrowded, and all the natives come out. It became a way to greet the New Year....a walk on the beach and dinner at a nice restaurant. We lived close enough that we could go home first to get presentable, change out of jeans and sneakers into something suitable for fine dining, and comb our windblown hair.

I've been removed from the beach for several years now. But I'm getting used to Pennsylvania. If you hear me bemoaning the loss of "my beach" just remind me of how beautiful the mountains are, and the clouds that float among them …. some of the most amazing clouds I've ever seen. I'm learning to love the country, too.

Beautiful Country Path in Early Spring

* * *

JIFFLE

There's no way in the world you could know what that means, unless you were a member of the Junior Fellowship League (J.F.L.) at the Swedish Lutheran Church in Brooklyn during the late 1940s and early '50s. Finding J.F.L. too annoying to pronounce, we preferred JIFFLE.

At first we were not an eclectic group. Most of us were first-generation Americans whose parents still spoke Swedish at home, especially when they didn't want us to know what they were talking about. We never did tell them that we understood most of it, even though we could only *speak* baby-Swedish after wending our way through the New York City school system. But most of us had friends outside church, from school or the neighborhood, and soon enough there were a few teenagers of various persuasions added to the mix.

All of our group went to City schools. Fort Hamilton High was co-ed and *the* desired destination, though some of us were out of the district. It sat majestic, high on a hill overlooking the Narrows, close to where the Verrazano Bridge is now. My parents decided that Bay Ridge High was the place for me, an all-girls' school located near our church. Many of the boys went to Brooklyn Tech, our "brother school," known for producing talented engineers. Bay Ridge was the parental choice because, aside from the academics, they thought that associating only with girls all day would keep me out of trouble. Dear, loving, naïve parents. They didn't know what a crowd of smart, revved up JIFFLE kids could do after school let out.

Not that we got into any *serious* trouble. It was back in the day when drugs were only for jazz drummers, though we girls knew we looked *tres* sophisticated with a cigarette between our fingers, and a few of the boys were crazy-macho with a pack of Camels rolled up in their tee shirt sleeves. Most of us looked like little kids playing grown-up, not that we realized it, but who cared when one was channeling his or her inner movie star.

Trouble was where one found it. I wasn't allowed to have a bicycle, the rationale being that bicycles were just too dangerous to ride on city streets. But the parents never saw me taking off on the handlebars of Max's bike. It was the best transportation to Confirmation class, since I rarely had a dime for the bus, and it was quite a distance to walk. Max was even braver than I was. He had to keep our balance while peering around me to watch for oncoming traffic.

My best friend, Cindy, lived on 103rd Street and I lived on 56th Street. As I mentioned, bus fare was in short supply, so we usually walked back and forth. You could do that at almost any time of the day or night without fear.

Cindy's parents were "progressive" and often let her invite the whole gang to their three room apartment. We would all take the elevator to the roof to watch the Coney Island fireworks in the summer.

 On one after midnight occasion, my friend Jon decided to walk me home, certainly concerned for my well-being, but also interested in possibly getting a goodnight kiss for his trouble, only to find my father waiting on the front stoop, and ready to explode. Poor Jon. His motives were mostly pure, but he got the brunt of Daddy's temper, and I got the only swat I ever received from either of my parents.

Our gang enjoyed the Sunday evening JIFFLE meetings at the church, and we would often present little theatricals of our own invention.

Tiny Lundqvist was a gentle giant, standing about six-two with a weight commensurate to his height. Tiny agreed to play Juliet to my Romeo, so we got him up on a ladder to simulate a balcony and then started searching for a suitable garment. The best we could come up with was the big brown cover that protected three huge coffee urns in the church kitchen. Tiny wasn't exactly adorable, but everyone enjoyed the show.

Our friend Jim decided we should produce an original musical, which he began to compose with help from his brother, Theo, a self-taught pianist. It was based on *The Legend of Sleepy Hollow*, and I kept the original, handwritten script for almost 30 years until I met Theo again at one of our JIFFLE reunions and gave it back to him.

My dear friend Jenny was particularly creative and liked to make interesting things for us on special occasions. I still treasure a diploma she made for me, though I don't remember why I was honored with this Major Award.

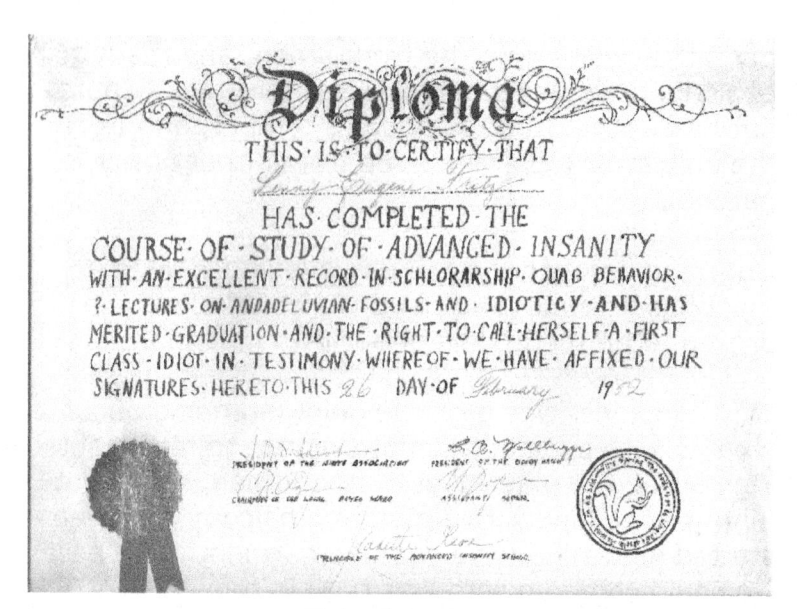

Major Award

We were fond of inventing commercials for real as well as made-up and improbable products, sometimes with accompanying jingles. The one that's been messing with my head for 65 years went like this: "Waterman's pens write under water. Waterman's pens squirt under water. Take swimming lessons to write your name. Waterman's pens will squirt again." Oh, my. We thought we were so clever.

Sometimes we enacted the commercials as part of a larger program. Terrible Tea is the one I remember best. Cindy would pick up an imaginary pitcher and ask, "Cream?" to which I, with imaginary cup and raised pinky, would reply, "Yes, then kyew." Then, an invisible sugar bowl with tiny imaginary sugar tongs. "Sugar?" "Two, then kyew." And now for the big yuck …. "Tea?" "No, then kyew." For some reason, this always got a big laugh. We were so delighted with ourselves that we would laugh at anything.

Occasionally we would get the urge to go dancing at Vasa Castle Hall way up in The Bronx. They always had good Scandinavian music played by real human beings. No recordings allowed! If the boys didn't want to go, some of us girls would get gussied up in our crinolines and dancing shoes and go by ourselves via subway. It was a long ride, but well worth it. The normally dour Swede can get rowdy listening to a hot accordion, especially when there's enough beer, and we always had a good time. Of course, we were too young to be drinking beer, so let's not talk about that.

I should probably mention how we would hitchhike from Fort Hamilton to Jones Beach on hot summer days. Two of the girls would stand at the side of the road with thumbs up. When someone stopped, two of the boys would jump out from behind the shrubbery and we would all pile into the stranger's car. Needless to say, the collective parents had no clue that this was going on, or we would all have been grounded for life.

I met my future husband at JIFFLE. I was a newbie, 14 and just confirmed, and he was 16 ½, an older man. He ran with the gang that was aging out of the group, and he was the only older kid who was ever willing to play shuffleboard with the younger ones. He went to Fort Hamilton High and so did Cindy.

Some best friend! She would tell me when she saw him in school talking with one girl or another. She knew I was madly in love and enjoyed rubbing it in.

I was a little kid and I knew I didn't have a chance
…. until I was almost 17 and we met again at a
party. Well, more about that another time, maybe.

Small JIFFLE House Party, author lower right

Even while our group was out having fun, church
was a big part of our life together. Our usual
meeting place was "at 1935," the cornerstone of
the church building, where the early arrivals would
lounge on the steps, waiting until everyone
eventually showed up. On Easter Sunday, before
dressing up for services, we would get ourselves
down to the beach to watch the sunrise and sing
hymns with the crowd gathered there to greet the
Risen Christ. And Christmas Eve became a
disappointment to many parents who were left to
their own devices as we chose to gather at one
home and then go off to the midnight service
together.

These halcyon days didn't last forever. We went
off to college, into the service, to jobs, but some of
us still saw each other after church, or for lunch in
the City, or to go shopping on a Saturday morning.
Sharon's parents had a little bungalow on a canal

in Long Beach, and occasionally a few of the girls would meet in Penn Station on a Friday summer's evening and take the train out to spend the weekend. Some of us were in each other's wedding parties, and many of us were guests at those weddings. Sometimes we had parties in our small apartments. But everyone kept in touch with someone, and friendships continued, although not on a daily basis as they had when we were younger.

Sometimes I wonder how we grew up with no major disasters, but we did, and the best part is that many of this group of once upon a time teens still get together every few years to catch up over a long weekend. We tried some Swedish dances when we met a few years ago at Myrtle Beach, but Max, my one-time favorite dancing partner, and I found that while the spirit was willing, the flesh was too weak for the rigors of the *hambo* and the *schottische*. But the waltz works, and we still remember what we once vowed would always true: "JIFFLE Forever!"

All Dressed Up on Easter Sunday
* * *

HAPPINESS

I just came across an old saying: "The happiness of your life depends on the quality of your thoughts. Therefore, guard accordingly" …. Marcus Aurelius. There's more to it (as you can tell by the little dots) but this is enough to start a discussion.

What makes you happy?

As we get older, this is a profound question and one that needs to be addressed sooner or later. My friend, Glenn, here at Lutherburgh knows exactly what makes him happy. He strives to make someone smile every day and his standard response to the question "How are you?" is "Mahvelous!" Marcus Aurelius would be proud.

Lately I've taken to keeping a gratitude journal. Every evening before turning out the light I jot down a few words about something I am grateful for this day. Looking back, I can see a few themes of happiness shining through.

At the top of the list of what makes me happy: interactions with my kids. They are very busy, so when I have the chance to visit with them or talk on the phone, it really makes my day. I even learned how to text to make communication easier which is a big deal for someone who is so desperately technology-challenged.

Doing things with friends is way up on my happy list. I love exploring my new environment here in Pennsylvania. Driving up hill and down dale on winding roads that dead-end unexpectedly is very exciting, and I'm grateful that I have friends who are willing to go along so I don't get lost forever. Thank goodness for my GPS. It may appear that I'm going someplace I don't want to go, but I always get there in the end.

Just *having* friends makes me enormously happy! I moved to Lutherburgh from Long Island not knowing a soul, and now I have several close friends and many friendly acquaintances. It doesn't get much better than that.

My gratitude diary shows me that I'm happy about having good food to eat even though I rarely prepare it myself anymore, and being healthy enough to attend exercise classes most days.

I'm really happy when I go to the theater and concerts here in the Valley, or in New York City, or in our own venue here at Lutherburgh.

There are simple pleasures that create happiness for me. I love to sit out on my balcony and watch the clouds forming and changing. This works well into the fall, when I can also watch the trees changing color in the woods across the way.

Climbing into bed on nights when nothing hurts is high on the happiness spectrum. So is waking up in the same condition! In fact, so is waking up at all! If I'm here for one more day there's probably something I need to do, so let's get to it.

Of course, there are things that make me unhappy, but I make an effort not to dwell on them. If I can do something about it, I do. Otherwise, I just try to let it go. When I'm really annoyed I call one of those good friends and unload. Sometimes I need to unload on two or three dear souls. By the time I'm done I usually feel a lot better.

Sometimes I get the feeling that life is closing in on me. Those are the times I most appreciate the little things that make me happy.

So I think Marcus Aurelius was onto something, and I'm grateful to him for calling it to my attention.

* * *

MENTAL MEANDERINGS

I'm always surprised at how much wisdom can be found in messages on tee shirts. Awhile back I found a message on a tee shirt that really impressed me: "Be Yourself; Everyone Else is Taken." Well, another one has surfaced which fits my present condition perfectly. It goes: "My Train of Thought Has Left the Station." So my plan is to wander randomly among my remaining brain cells and see what develops.

I read recently that senior citizens who don't think of themselves as being as old as they really are live longer than people who think they are older than they really are. If this is true I expect to live much longer than I want to, because my unconscious has come to the surface and told me that I'm actually 18. This isn't too much of a surprise, since I've noticed that over the past few years I've been acting more and more like a teenager. What do you suppose that means?

Something I've been mulling over lately is my bucket list. Last year I crossed off bungee jumping, not because I ever got around to it, but because I finally figured out that a sharp snap to a body older than 30 or so while flying through space could be detrimental to one's health.

Zip lining is on hold for the time being although I'm not ready to abandon the idea entirely. The last time I wanted to try it I was confronted by a very high telephone pole with about 10 metal rungs pounded into it like a stepladder. To get off the zip line, it was necessary to climb down those rungs and then, somehow, climb out of the leather sling you climbed into before heading down the mountain. Now I don't know about you, but I was not going to give that a try!

About five years ago, when I was visiting my friend on Cape Cod, we decided to go to a nearby park that featured a wonderful merry-go-round. It's located in a building that used to be a roundhouse, the ride is free, and you can circle around all day long if you want to …. and if you're not prone to motion sickness. The last time I had been on that merry-go-round was 1982 or '83, so I was really looking forward to it. The problem was, when I stood next to the horse I wasn't able to get my leg over it, never mind climbing into the saddle. That forced me to think again about zip lines, and I may never get up the nerve to find out what it feels like to soar through the air like an eagle.

Two of my goals since moving to Lutherburgh were to learn about football and opera. I haven't gotten anywhere with football, even though I've sat through the Super Bowl games here two or three times. I really like the pizza and beer, but I have no idea what's going on with the game and only cheer when one of my friends tells me it's time to start the fist-pumping and hollering. This helps me feel like part of the crowd, but it doesn't make the game any easier to understand.

Opera is coming along nicely, though. I've found some music-savvy friends who are willing to give me a synopsis before the show starts and answer any questions I might have. My problem with opera is cognitive dissonance. If you're not familiar with the term, it refers to a situation involving conflicting attitudes, beliefs or behaviors. I suffer from this big time when I watch a short, tubby guy in a velvet robe playing Othello, being adored by the beautiful soprano who swears her undying love and fidelity ….. while he scorns her. This makes absolutely no sense to me, but I've found it all looks better if I squint. On second thought, maybe tubby Othello *knows* how short and round he is, and that's why he doubts the beautiful ingénue's devotion.

By the way, if you haven't been on a merry-go-round lately I want you to know that sitting on a bench next to a wooden swan in no way compares to riding a gallant steed up and down as the music goes 'round and 'round.

* * *

WORKING

"Wukkin, wukkin, wukkin," baby Steven would say, when I asked him where Daddy was. All of us developed a strong work ethic early on, and I thought it would be interesting to figure out how many jobs I've had in my life. It's going to be hard, since there were a lot of them.

The very first time I ever earned money for my efforts was when I was ten. The couple who owned the candy store around the corner, where we went to make our telephone calls, had a daughter who was about five. Her parents paid me 25 cents for an afternoon's worth of entertaining her while they both worked in the store. She was pretty energetic, but we stayed in the store, or just outside the door, the whole time so her folks were always within reach. That was probably the least stressful job I ever had.

After that I experienced a period of unemployment until about age 15 when I applied for working papers so I could get a summer job. It was at a local bank and all day long I sat in front of an enormous adding machine. I looked like I was playing the slots, pulling the handle as I went through a stack of checks and entered them on lengths of paper tape. My right arm developed quite a muscle that summer, and I thought I would die of boredom. However, I did have cash in my pocket which was the only reason I wanted a job anyway.

The next summer I got work thanks to my cousin who was a private secretary for an executive at a large corporation in downtown Manhattan. I was the office gofer, running paperwork from the main office on Broad Street to a satellite office a few blocks away. That was a great job. I got plenty of exercise when the weather was fine, and money for the subway when it was bad. And no one paid attention to the time I left and the time I returned. During lunch hours I took a turn at the switchboard to relieve the operator, and that was great fun, plugging wires into the board after answering the phone in my best, professional, secretarial voice.

Two years later and graduated from high school I decided that one semester at Brooklyn College was enough. (Tuition-free; how dumb was that?) My boyfriend and I would get married after he returned from his tour of duty with the Army in Japan. So I took a three-month business course at the YWCA on Lexington Avenue and went to work in the typing pool of another large corporation.

It's a good thing typing pools don't exist anymore. B o o o o r ing! I sat at one typewriter in a row of many, pecking away at whatever the supervisor handed me. At the time I was typing about 80 words a minute so I got through a lot of work every day. It got old fast, but I was soon rescued by a young executive who needed a private secretary ….. his first. We hit it off right away and remained friends until he passed away a few years ago. So I became a secretary in the advertising department and loved that job, staying with it until I got married and became pregnant and too uncomfortable to ride the subway from Brooklyn to Manhattan anymore.

Of course, I had to quit. Women didn't go back to work after having children back then, unless they *really* had to. At least, none of the women in my circle did, but then, none of us had a serious career to go back to.

Soon my husband and I decided it was time to move out of Brooklyn. The day we found our dream house, a little ranch in a development in central Long Island that hadn't even been built yet, I worried all the way home that we might have made a mistake in putting down the non-refundable five dollar deposit that would reserve the plot of land we wanted!

Dream House on Long Island

A year later we moved in, counting every penny but ecstatic about our new home. One day I was reading the local neighborhood newspaper and they were looking for someone to write the Deer Park "gossip" section, so I dressed Steven up and trotted down to the office where I was immediately hired to write from home, one column a week, delivered every Monday. The pay was miniscule, but it was all mine, the only personal funds I'd had since before the little guy was born.

Baby David arrived, and I was still able to find enough time to prepare my column every week, and that job lasted awhile. Our financial situation had improved by then, so the pittance I had been contributing wasn't really needed. I got interested in church work and volunteered for most of the time I would have spent in regular employment, until I got itchy for "real" work and was recruited by a friend to become a Welcome Wagon hostess in the early 70s. That was a fun job!

I looked up Welcome Wagon on the internet the other day, and it seems to have changed, along with the rest of the world, since I worked there. My job was to show up at new residents' homes with a basket of goodies to help them get acquainted with their new neighborhood.

The company I knew was a family-owned business out of Memphis, Tennessee, and was a well-run and very professional organization. When I was hired I had to attend a week of training at the Manhattan office. I was late the first day because of problems on the Long Island Railroad. I saw this as a bad omen and was ready to quit before I started, but common sense prevailed and, back home again, I was part of a cadre of hostesses serving almost every town on Long Island. I loved visiting with the newcomers. One year I was able to participate in our town's 4th of July parade with a Welcome Wagon basket tied to the roof of my car. What fun!

Welcome Wagon in the Parade

I became a manager and went to train for a week at the main office in Memphis. It was an exciting time! I was away from home, on my own, for the first time in what seemed like centuries. Every afternoon the trainees, from all across the country, were called in to the board room where we met for a short period of relaxation with the dowager who was president of the company during which we indulged in "Co Cola," as Madam President called it, and cookies.

Sometime later the Memphis family decided to sell the company and I wasn't ready for the change. So I found myself a job at a newly-established advertising agency in the next town and worked as their secretary/receptionist for a few years. (This was where I worked when I stopped smoking.)

One of the best things about that job was their openness to experimentation, meaning that they let me try my hand at writing copy. My biggest achievement was doing a series of ads for a carpet company.

I left there when a friend asked me to come and work with her for a young local attorney. That was an interesting job. Automatic typewriters were just coming out and it was part of my job to program all kinds of boilerplate clauses into the machines. I still can't believe I did that! You've heard what happens to me when I'm confronted with any kind of technology.

Jean and I enjoyed our work at the law office. Our desks were facing each other so we could chat in between client visits. We would put on the coffee pot in the morning and drink coffee all day long.

About this time home life began to deteriorate, so I quit the job I enjoyed and went to another small law firm where I was able to work only four hours a day. But I was in a bad place emotionally and started making mistakes. One of those mistakes infuriated the client, and rightly so. I got fired.

I had been working on a bachelor's degree in Community and Human Services through Empire State College at Stony Brook University and applied myself as best as I could to finishing the program. I began to understand that a divorce was probably going to form my future, and I needed a job that paid a living wage. A degree would open that door.

In the meantime I had to work. My pastor came through. He was in conversation with the director of a Lutheran school and persuaded him that he needed a woman on the executive staff of an institution that was solidly male. This time my old advertising background came into play. I was in charge of all the public relations and publicity for the school: all kinds of written material, newspaper ads, letters to area churches touting the school, recruitment brochures, alumni contacts, anything and everything. I soon discovered that the written word needed enhancing with pictures, so I joined a camera club, acquired a friend who had been a newspaper cameraman, and did some nice work.

I had a great title, Director of Institutional Advancement, but that job came to an end when the director who had hired me got fired. I was "laid off" along with him. I was scared.

In between the jobs with the attorney and the school I had moved out of my home and into a studio apartment in a private house in the next town. There was no way I could stay comfortably in my home once I started divorce proceedings. But I needed to be working!

I was saved once again, at least for the time being. One of the people I had been in contact with for the school was the area manager of a church-related insurance company, and he persuaded me to give it a try. For a year I made good money selling something I believed in, but I was having trouble with the late night hours that were necessary for visiting with both wives and husbands. I was thinking about quitting when a potential client met me at the door with a snootful of alcohol and began to curse me for taking advantage of church members. I quit the next day. The manager was kind. He suggested I take a month off, with pay, to gather myself together again, but at the end of the month I knew I was done selling life insurance.

My divorce came through and I moved back into my home again, my "real house" as I had continued to call it during my exile. Now it was more important than ever that I get a job that paid a decent salary. There was a local company nearby advertising for secretaries and I was hired to be the administrative assistant to the vice president for advertising. This was an easy job to get. The CEO of the organization had a reputation for making unwanted advances to his young secretaries, and women didn't want to work there. Since I was in my 50s and therefore not likely to seem attractive to this man, I got the job easily. It was fun to be back in advertising again, and I could concentrate on my studies and graduate with a Bachelor's degree in Community and Human Services.

The degree got me a job at a displaced homemaker center where a staff of seven dedicated women worked toward helping others who had been "displaced" from their homemaking jobs through various life circumstances. I *loved* that job and stayed there for eleven years.

Women would come in, worried and discouraged, not knowing how they would be able to take care of themselves, and our staff would provide clerical training and preparation for the workplace with a series of workshops, some of which we prepared and presented ourselves, and others presented by people like C.P.A.s, psychotherapists, domestic violence professionals, etc.

Some of the staff presentations dealt with the practical issues of job seeking: understanding the want ads, writing a resume, dressing for an interview, and some that were just motivational. Each of us had our favorite ways of encouraging our clients to take charge of their lives. For example, I insisted that no one on the premises called herself or her peers "girls" or "ladies." We were all "WOMEN" in that office. I also liked to spend some time on things like standing straight and walking tall, a bit of what might be called "attitude" today.

At the end of every semester we would have a party, with everyone bringing in one of their favorite dishes (with recipes if available). One talented woman in the winter class of '94 presented each staff member with a poem/certificate written especially for her. This was mine, and 20 years later I'm still very proud of it.

Helen

"WOMEN," you say,
"Stand up tall."
"Oh, but Helen," we say,
"That ought not be all..."

We struggled and worked
Through winters and gales.
But we WOMEN are strong
And therefore prevailed.

You should be proud
Of the WOMEN you see.
'Cause WOMEN we are...
And WOMEN we'll be.

WINTER CLASS OF '94

That was my absolutely favorite job. When I obtained my Master's in Social Work I wanted to be able to counsel our clients and couldn't do it because there wasn't anyone in our part of the agency who had the credentials to supervise me.

Steven and David with M.S.W. Mom

So I left there to take a job at a mental health agency for which I wasn't prepared. My two internships had been in drug and alcohol counseling and domestic violence, but I had no practical experience in mental health. I was transferred to another branch of the agency where I stayed for about a year, until a great opportunity presented itself.

I had been working part-time evenings for the domestic violence agency where I had done my internship and had come to know most of the workers in the field. It was a small community. About a year and a half before I was scheduled to retire I was offered a position at one of those domestic violence agencies and enjoyed going to various senior citizen centers with the goal of finding and assisting any seniors who might be experiencing abuse in their homes.

When I took the job I intended to work until I was 70 or so, but the travel (25 miles each way to the office and many more miles daily to the senior centers) got to me and I called it quits after two years. Things had gone well there, and I was called back twice to fill in for a few months at a time during vacancies. I also worked part-time in a bridal shop. Mothers of the brides and grooms were my specialty, but the prom girls were challenging and lots of fun to work with.

When Ed died, eight years after I retired, I needed to find a new place to live. I anticipated moving to Lutherburgh but wasn't quite ready. An amazing coincidence allowed me to work as pastoral assistant at my Lutheran church with a little house to live in for four years, while I was getting ready for Pennsylvania.

Now I do some volunteer work at Lutherburgh and at my new Lutheran church downtown.

I've always liked "wukkin" and plan to do so until I just can't anymore.

* * * *

LEAVING HOME

One summer evening, when Steven was about three, my husband and I were watching the late night news on television when the phone rang. That was scary. The phone never rang late at night unless something was very wrong.

It was our across-the-backyard neighbor, who had become beloved Aunt Kathleen to Steven. "Hey," she said, "do you know where your son is?" "He's been in bed for hours," I replied. "Why?" "What kind of a mother are you?" Kathleen asked. "He's in my kitchen, having milk and cookies."

Evidently Steven had awakened in the night and headed for our kitchen where he found the back screen door unlocked. He was unperturbed when we ran across the yard to get him. "Thanks for the cookies, Aunt Kathleen," he said as he cheerfully waved goodbye.

David had one episode of wandering when he was about 4. He left the house by the front door while my husband was in the basement and I was in our bedroom. When I realized that the front door was wide open I called downstairs to find my husband still there, then checked the boys' rooms and discovered that David was missing.

Today I might have thought of kidnapping, but that night I just thought I had another wanderer. After some minutes of calling and beating the bushes we found him, fast asleep, under the crabapple tree in the front yard. He never did wake up when we

Sleepwalkers in the Daylight

carried him back to his bed, but the next day we put hooks and chains across the top of the front and back doors, and we never forgot to hook them once we were in for the night.

* * *

ON BEING A SNOWBIRD

In 2004, after a little cancer operation, (which was successful, so don't worry) I decided that I needed to grab life by the hair and do something exciting and wildly unlike my usual self. That turned out to be buying a double-wide at a senior citizens' trailer park in Florida. This trailer was firmly anchored to the ground and going nowhere, and I came by it due to the love and care of friends Betsy and Joe who also lived at the Five Seasons Senior Community Trailer Park. *Five* seasons? Don't ask.

Joe called one hot June afternoon to tell us about this wonderful opportunity. Ed wanted nothing to do with it, but I decided that a trip to Florida in June was just what I needed. The trailer in question was right next door to Betsy's and Joe's, but as it turned out, it had already been purchased before I had gotten on the plane. But Joe told me that there was another one down the road that was available.

It wasn't easy to find a vacancy at Five Seasons, but these two trailers were for sale for the same reason. Their owners had been growing pot in their spare bedrooms. What an occupation for a couple of senior citizens! These were evidently very sophisticated operations with all the growing being done hydroponically. One of the neighbors tipped off the cops when he realized that even though the temperature outside was 101 degrees, no air conditioners were running in two of the bedrooms. The owners were at home, so something peculiar was going on.

Florida Trailer

I wish I had been there to see the raid. My new next-door neighbor explained to me that when she came home from the Hard Rock Café late one evening, police were all over the lawn and people were being removed in handcuffs. That my neighbor was at the Hard Rock Café was interesting in itself, since she was 97 years old at the time, weighed about 90 lbs., and looked like she might evaporate at any minute. But she did enjoy an occasional evening at the tables.

The trailer (by now I was calling it a manufactured home) cost me a lot more than I should have paid for it, in many ways. I was bedazzled by the view from the Florida room in the back. It looked out on a canal and there were posts out back which I discovered later were left over from a little dock that had floated away years before. It was frequented by water birds, and I loved watching the anhinga drying their wings in the breeze.

Desirable Water View

The owners were leaving behind a glass-topped coffee table supported by two big plaster fish. I saw this as an especially good omen since my zodiac sign is Pisces. There was also a brand new, top-of-the-line washer which must have come from the proceeds of marijuana sales, with an antique but useable dryer, both hidden behind a set of louvered doors.

My eyes glazed over as I imagined how the place would look once I had finished with it. Porch furniture in the Florida room, bright pillows, lots of flowers planted outside. Whoopee! It would be like furnishing a dollhouse, but a lot more expensive, as it turned out. Well, I gave them the money the next day (now you have to get an inspection, just like a real house, and a lawyer, too) and sealed the deal by transferring two motor home stickers from their name to mine.

Fortunately I had to go home right away, or I would, perhaps, have jumped into the canal and fed myself to the alligators. The former owners disappeared the next day, and buyer's remorse was useless. Maybe another time I'll tell you what went into making it a home.

* * *

THE DESTRUCTION OF TEAKETTLES

Perhaps I should begin by saying that, although I've experienced a few disasters that included teakettles, I'm not a tea-drinker by nature, upbringing, or disposition.

I was raised in a Swedish household only lightly touched by American customs, and tea was not a part of our everyday lifestyle. We drank coffee morning, noon, and night, and I had my first cup when I was about four years old. Tea was an exotic and seldom-used commodity. It was good for one purpose, and one purpose only …… medicinally. My mother considered it exceptionally effective for easing coughs, especially when laced with honey and lots of lemon, and also when recuperating from any kind of stomach ailment. My father, too, found it good for digestive upsets, but only if mixed with rye whiskey and downed with 10 black peppercorns. I never questioned where that recipe came from, but as far as I knew it worked. As I grew older and more familiar with the kitchen and its contents I began to wonder about the peppercorns, but mine was not to question parental wisdom, merely to disregard it when it had to do with me.

Even though we didn't indulge in tea-drinking very often, we always had a teakettle. Since our use was so limited, I suspect we could have done without it all together, boiling the water in an ordinary saucepan when necessary, but my mother had spent her first years in America as a maid in a wealthy home, and she knew how things ought to be done. So when my husband and I got married, one of our gifts from my parents was a beautiful, imported teakettle. I believe it was actually made in Norway, not Sweden, but as I've mentioned before, this could be forgiven when the stakes were high.

 It was a magnificent teakettle! It was large and bright red, made of some kind of metal that seemed to glow golden from deep within the red surface. I cherished that kettle. It sat proudly on the stove day after day, often untouched except when I wiped off the particles of cooking spatter that occasionally marred its perfection. I loved it so much that I insisted the kettle was mine when my husband and I divorced. I took it with me to the small apartment I rented while waiting for our legal work to be completed, and then it went with me to my friend Linny's house where I lived for several months.

Linny was a dear friend (still is), but she has always been "distracted" and I've often wondered how she has managed all these years to get anything done at all. Anyway, one day I came home from work to find my beautiful kettle in ruins. Linny had decided to make tea, and she forgot about the kettle boiling away while she did the day's crossword puzzle. This was 30 years after I had been given the kettle, and I had no idea how to replace it, or even if it were possible to do so. After that we used Linny's battered old kettle, which we should have done in the first place if I had been thinking clearly, and when I left her home I bought another strictly utilitarian kettle for myself.

Some years later, after I moved to Ed's house, I saw a kettle in a catalog and decided it was worthy to take the place of my dear departed red one. This one was sparkling white enamel, and it had a little bird perched on the end of the spout that whistled when the water began to boil. What a great kettle!

One day Ed, an enthusiastic tea drinker, put the kettle on to boil and then went outside to check on his tomato plants. When I came home and noticed it was missing from its usual place on the stove, Ed sheepishly removed it from the trash. There was the pretty little birdy melted into an ugly lump and the white enamel turned a noxious gray.

When I moved to Lutherburgh I decided to buy myself a blue kettle with a metal base, which I kept on my stove where I could admire it when I happened to think about it at all. Sadly, this grew a white crust around the bottom edge and had to be deep-sixed.

Beautiful New Teakettle

But lucky for me, one of the many catalogs I thumbed through featured a lovely stainless steel kettle, made in England, not too big, with a pretty curved spout and priced just right.

It arrived this afternoon, and I hope that this one will last as long as I do.

* * *

ABOUT ED

Ed was my partner for 16 years and my friend for longer than that. He was an original, a one-and-only, and as it turned out, exactly the right person for me in my mature years. This might seem odd, since he was 17 years older than I, but it took me a while to find out how old he was because he was so active and energetic.

When I first met Ed I felt sorry for him. He was a big, muscular guy, but he had no right arm. I learned later that he had been shot in a hunting accident when he was about twelve and had lost the arm at the shoulder as a result. It was a devastating situation for a young, active boy, who had lost his mother not long before, but it seems he learned to make the best of it by playing soccer instead of baseball and managing the football team in high school. He was the only child in his family of four boys and two girls who was sent to college and he wasn't eligible for the draft so did his service working for an aerospace company.

I was divorced, he was a widower when we had our first date. Before long we were spending lots of time together and eventually he decided that we ought to live together. Note that *he* decided; I wasn't so sure. I was old fashioned enough not to feel quite right about living with a man without being married, but I knew that marriage could bring a raft of trouble for people our age with adult children to consider. And we were both stubborn, opinionated, and used to doing our own thing. Could it possibly work out?

Well, it took six years for Ed to convince me. I kept stalling. I suggested he move in with me, knowing that he would never do that. He loved his neighbors and they loved him so I'd have to move there. Ed was a "collector of many interesting things" as his sons and I described him in his obituary, and there was no way I was going to live in his house unless he did a major cleanup and some much needed renovations. I never expected him to do any of it, but I was amazed at what the place looked like when he was done: a brand new kitchen with new appliances and cabinets; a beautiful picture window in the upstairs bedroom flanked by two nice chairs so we could look out at his big backyard and watch the leaves turn and the snow fall. There were closets galore and everything glowed with fresh paint. My excuses were running out.

Finally I decided I might as well just do it, since it became clear that he was not giving up, and I was finding it harder and harder to keep up my own house. I put my place on the market, started packing and sorting 40 years or so of the stuff that one accumulates over time, and prepared to make a commitment. My house sold faster than I expected, so I moved before all of Ed's cleaning out had been done. His garage, which was supposed to be for *my* car since I had to leave my garage attached to the house which was no longer mine, was still the resting place for many of his collected items. Not good. But my buyers were waiting and I had to move *now*.

Since we weren't going to get married we couldn't have a pre-nuptial agreement, but I had heard that people were making "living together" contracts. We needed one, for sure, since we were different in some significant ways, so we negotiated our way through an agreement (which neither of us ever got around to signing), and jumped in. My pastor said he was sorry, but there was no such thing as a Lutheran commitment ceremony, which we both would have liked. He did agree to come and bless the house. It was a lovely rite from the Book of Occasional Services, and I still have the candle we used as we went from room to room, blessing each one in turn.

It turned out to be fun, most of the time, living with Ed. Even at his age he still had that hard-muscled strong left arm and it served him well. He climbed trees to cut dead limbs, climbed ladders to muck out the gutters, carted loads of topsoil to plant his vegetable garden, mowed the big lawn regularly, helped the neighbors with their gardening chores, moved furniture as needed, joined the walking club at the Senior Center and did all the food shopping. You only had to be with Ed for a few day before you forgot that he had only one arm.

Ed was an avid gardener. There were massive flowering shrubs near the front door and alongside the fence which he cultivated carefully. The vegetable garden was his pride and his delight, and we both enjoyed growing tomatoes, zucchini, eggplant and peppers. All of these could be made into a delicious *ratatouille* which we enjoyed all summer.

Ed

The thing I liked best about us was that we could argue and still be friends. My husband wouldn't fight. He'd just leave the house and the discussion was ended before it began. Ed and I could yell at each other and stomp our feet and still make up before the day was over.

Food shopping was one of the things we argued about. Entenmann's Bakery was located in the next town, and they had a fabulous thrift store on the premises. Ed would load up on coffee cakes, donuts, and chocolate chip cookies, sometimes coming home with 16 or 20 boxes. Maybe it was his substitute for collecting things like old TVs but it drove me crazy. First we had to find a place to keep all that, and I wasn't supposed to eat it anyway, even though I really liked it, so I was in a constant state of frustrated gastronomical temptation.

Another thing that drove me nuts was his lack of interest in cleaning out the garage. We had many words over that, but it finally happened. One of my best friends lived two blocks away, and the trash collectors visited us on the same day. My friend Chris and I devised a plan. Every week or so I would take one item from the back of our garage and leave it at the curb in front of Chris's house for trash collection. It wasn't too long before Ed caught on, but I had already disposed of several things and he realized I was serious, so he finished the job himself.

I was still working but Ed had retired some years earlier. He had a keen mind and was interested in almost everything, spending a lot of time at the public library reading and researching the things that fascinated him. When Betsy and Joe were visiting us from Florida we spent a day in Manhattan and lost Ed in the New York Public Library. They were getting ready to close and he was nowhere in sight. We finally picked him up in the genealogy section with a stack of books around him.

Perhaps it was the fact that he grew up during the Depression, but Ed was known to be frugal, occasionally beyond what I considered reasonable. But there were always ways to compensate. When a pipe burst under the floor beneath the hot water heater he wasn't ready to call the plumber. Instead, he rallied a few of our younger neighbors who knew at least a little more about it than he did, and together they tackled the problem. I just packed a bag and moved to Linny's house until I got the all clear.

Ed loved a party even more than I did. It was his birthday, Memorial Day, when I moved into his house and that Christmas we had a big party for the neighbors. They were dumbfounded when they saw the new look and he really enjoyed playing host. Our first Thanksgiving together we hosted the dinner for Ed's side of the family. He was happy and that made me happy, too. We continued to have a lot of company, even when he was in hospice care at home. And he was always ready to welcome my women friends who certainly couldn't be ignored just because I was in a relationship.

Ed enjoyed travel, too. He had done quite a lot of traveling before we met, but we had trips together to Scandinavia, Israel and Egypt, and from Florida to Maine.

Ed in Egypt

One of the things I most liked about living with Ed was cooking for him. Back then I was a good cook, and he enjoyed everything, was willing to try anything new, and was kind if he didn't like what I put in front of him. He would never say he didn't like it. He would say, "Maybe we don't have to have that again?" And he always said thank you.

Toward the end of his life he was in and out of the hospital and rehab, but Ed used his time wisely. One day when I visited in rehab he handed me a chart showing where each of the vegetable plants was to go and told me where to find the phone number for the county extension service. I received elaborate instructions on how to select the soil from the vegetable garden for testing. I got the garden planted and soon after that he came home with hospice care.

He chose to stay in the second floor bedroom that overlooked the garden. When the zucchini and cucumbers started to grow I would point them out and wave them in the air when I picked them. He was on a feeding tube and couldn't enjoy them as he used to, but he liked to see what was happening in his garden. It was still *his* garden.

I often think of how much Ed would have enjoyed living at Lutherburgh. He was a real people person and liked to keep active for as long as he was able. But the funny thing was, he would never have agreed to move here. So he had his wish and died at home, with all of us around him.

Ed was special, an original, a one-and-only. I was very blessed to have him in my life and I thank God for him every day.

* * *

Early Days

15 Years Later

WHERE DID THE SOCKS GO THIS TIME?

When I wrote about the disappearing socks awhile back I had no idea that a sequel would be necessary. However, the goings and comings of a few more of my personal belongings has pretty much required further consideration.

Just a few weeks ago a pretty crystal window hanging, about two inches long, fell from my bedroom window. I noticed this when I found the hook lying on the windowsill. The crystal was nowhere in sight. I'm very fond of that crystal. It has moved with me four times, and I've found it on the windowsill from time to time at each home, always ready to be put back up on the glass.

Of course I searched the floor, and as far under the bed as I could safely go. The crystal is faceted, not round, so it couldn't have rolled very far when it fell. I looked for many minutes, but it was gone.

I was reasonably sure that it wasn't *really* gone, but only, as I mentioned last time, resting in the alternate universe until the cosmic realignment of space and time brought it back. A week or so later it reappeared on my night table, in a place where it couldn't possibly have bounced when it fell off the window.

A second encounter with the unknown occurred recently when I lost my seldom-used cell phone. Again I searched, but for a longer period of time, dismantling every one of my handbags (I don't have that many, but it takes time), since that was the most likely place I would have left it. No luck. I couldn't find it.

I went to the phone store to see about disconnecting the phone so that no dishonest person who happened to find it could make calls to the far reaches of Outer Mongolia. I discovered that no outgoing calls had been made in several days. This was encouraging news, so I put the account on hold and went home to search some more. Two days later the phone turned up in a back pocket of the white handbag I had just reactivated for summer use.

You might wish to argue that I had put it there myself and just forgotten I did it. If so, why was it not working anymore? Obviously, it had entered the alternate universe and either been zapped by light rays or injured by someone/thing who didn't know how to use it.

The phone is working now, thanks to the intervention of a phone store clerk who pushed the "on" icon, which leads me to conclude that it didn't work due to a senior citizen brain burp on my part. Unfortunately that weakens my argument as to where the phone went, but as the old saying goes: "My mind is made up. Don't confuse me with the facts."

This mystery led, however, to a new line of inquiry about where the socks went, and *why* did they go? More importantly why, when most things ultimately return from the alternate universe, socks never do ….. at least mine never do. Do yours?

A few Lutherburghers have told me about their experiences with disappearing socks. Our neighbor Marge had 17 single socks in various dresser drawers when her children were still living at home. Another neighbor thinks at least a dozen of hers have gone missing over time.

What do the Alternate Universarians do with our socks? My thinking is that these entities must be quite different from humans so there's no chance we'll ever know why they want them; but speculation is interesting.

What value do they place on socks so that they never come back, when other items eventually do? Perhaps there's a kind of monetary value to socks. Are Marianne's socks worth 100 "whatevers," while mine are worthless? Is that why they never come back?

 Are my socks the alternate universe equivalent to the pennies we throw into the cup next to the Gift Shop cash register?   I think it would be a friendly gesture to donate my old socks with the holes in them, but I can't figure out how to go about it. The holes might make them even more valuable, but then again, the holey ones have never disappeared.

Or perhaps socks are like dessert in the alternate universe. Maybe the white athletic socks are equivalent to vanilla frozen yoghurt, while the more exotic colors equal cream puffs or double chocolate fudge pies. After all, anything is possible. Or maybe socks have some critical function related to alternate universe war, or maybe even sex …. but that would be weird.

If you think you know what it is about socks, why don't you let me know? I'd be truly grateful!

* * *

GADGETS

My definition of a gadget is something that solves a problem you didn't necessarily know you had until you happened to see the gadget. It should have two other characteristics: at least one moving part and a price of $10 or less. If the item is missing any of these things it should really be called a thingy, but the term gadget will do, and whether it's a gadget or a thingy, you must actually hand over your hard-earned money to obtain it.
The price factor is very important to me because I have a weakness for gadgets and have to hold tight to my credit cards when I find one that seems particularly interesting. The moving parts are just for fun.

I had high hopes for my latest purchase and for a short time those hopes were fulfilled, but one day the whole thing went south. This gadget was an egg cooker (only $10) and I was pretty sure it would work as advertised, so I bought this egg-shaped plastic thingy about eight inches high and six inches around with two inserts that looked like some kind of thin metal. The egg opens horizontally in the middle. The metal tray across the bottom section has several small holes plus four indentations to hold up to four eggs, and the top portion is lined with the same metal. Both metal pieces are removable.

The idea is to fill the bottom of the egg with water up to the metal, place one, two, three or four eggs in the indentations, fit the top of the egg in place over the bottom piece, put it in the microwave, time it according to directions for soft or hard-cooked eggs and turn on the microwave.

The first few times I used this little beauty I got four perfectly hard-cooked eggs. On another try I had a just right soft boiled egg for breakfast. The next time, not so good.

Each time I used the gadget I had a little more trouble fitting the top piece tightly to the bottom. Trying again for another breakfast egg, I was surprised when the top blew right off the plastic egg while it was being microwaved. I let the egg keep cooking, which was a mistake. When I took it out of the microwave and attempted to cut off the top the egg exploded!

Well, you may remember my story about washing pea soup off the side of the refrigerator. This wasn't nearly as bad, especially since the egg turned out to be well cooked. If it had staying soft boiled as I intended it would have been a lot worse. So I think that's the end of that gadget, even though it burns me to throw away a $10 item that's had so little use. I may have to give it one more try before I heave it into the trash.

Another gadget that did me wrong is an egg slicer. On reflection, it appears that most of my gadgets are kitchen-related even though I do very little cooking these days. When I bought this egg slicer I already had one, and I should have left well enough alone.

The "old" one is some kind of metal, rather heavy, and over time it's taken on a nasty, gray color, but it does a fine job slicing eggs. Then I saw a pretty white plastic one in the kitchen shop and decided to retire the old one. O beauty, how shallow thou art! The pretty plastic slicer lasted only a few months before falling apart. Thank goodness I hung on to the old gray mare. She's still bravely slicing eggs for me, and just like all the old folks around here, she can hold her place among the cute youngsters any time.

Another gadget I can't live without is my "Round Tuit." I'm sure you have one, too. It's a round piece of rubbery material that works wonders when I need to open a stubborn jar or bottle top. I have one that was a gift from the Bank of Smithtown and has been in my possession for more years than I care to remember.

Recently I needed to open a jar of pickles and couldn't find my Round Tuit. I searched the drawer where it has resided since I moved to Lutherburgh. I even searched the other kitchen drawers and finally took the first one completely apart. There was no Round Tuit in there. I shared this frustration with a few friends in hopes of glomming one from someone who had two, and when Nancy went to the market the next day she returned with several square pieces of purple plastic that worked almost as well.

The other day I went looking for my new, purple, square plastic substitute Round Tuit and there was the old one, right underneath it. I should have known that it would be in the alternate universe awaiting the appropriate time to stage a comeback. But since alternate universe time flow is unknown to me, I didn't want to just hang out waiting for my Tuit to come home.

Another thingy that I can't live without is a kitchen scrubby. I have to go to the Methodist Church Fall Bazaar every October to restock my supply of scrubbies. One talented woman there knits them out of some kind of plastic string, and they work wonders on dirty pots and pans, and they don't ever scratch! This year I bought six, and that should last me until next October.

One more gadget that, strictly speaking, isn't really a gadget but was too appealing to ignore cost me a lot more than I wanted to spend. So far I've never used it, and I probably never will. It doesn't have any moving parts, either, and I definitely didn't realized I needed one until I saw it.

I had seen this first in a catalog. I'm not quite sure what to call it. It's made of heavy metal and looks like a cookie sheet with a dozen depressions, each designed like a miniature bundt pan. I understood it was meant to make truffles, but I thought it would be fun to bake itty bitty bundt cakes of different flavors and put pretty toppings on them. "How hard could it be?" I asked myself. And how nice those little tiny cakes would be for a tea party.

As usual, the creative side of my brain was way ahead of the practical side, which didn't remind me until I had paid the clerk that I have never hosted a tea party in my life.

Some Gadgets and Thingies

There were detailed instructions on the packaging for making truffles, which I immediately discarded on the basis that I would never make them anyway. Then I started thinking about how much shortening would have to be applied into the nooks and crannies of the tiny bundt cake molds in order to free them from the pan when baking was done.

That was entirely too much thinking, and the pan remains in my oven drawer, unused to this day. Someday I really will have nothing else to do, and maybe I'll bake a batch of teeny tiny bundt cakes and have that tea party after all.

Last but not least is my picker-upper. This is a stick, about two feet long, with a magnet and pincers at the end which I tend to forget about much of the time. This had been Ed's picker-upper and he used it often and deftly, while I had a tendency to reach up for something, stretch too far, grab wildly for the item I wanted and wind up with several things scattered around my feet. Once I realized how unproductive that system was, I was happy to borrow the picker-upper from time to time.

But this item became essential when I had cataract surgery. The primary instruction after the procedure is "Don't bend over; the head must stay above the heart." This instruction is easier to give than to follow.

I'm not prone to dropping things as a rule, but after the surgery I became afflicted with the dropsies big time. I dropped an uncapped bottle of expensive vitamins; I dropped a can of soup after I had opened it; I dropped my toothbrush; I dropped my hairbrush. I have never in my life been so grateful for any gadget!

So the moral of this story is, if you think you may need a gadget (and it doesn't cost more than $10) just go ahead and buy it. You won't be sorry!

* * *

WHAT DO YOU DO WITH A BOOMBA?

"Boomba" is a word you may never have heard unless you are of Pennsylvania Dutch extraction. I had never heard of it until moving to the Lehigh Valley, where the fine art of the Boomba seems to be dying out.

My friends Judith and Bill were ardent boomba fans in their younger days, and when they learned that I was a boomba virgin they invited me to attend a session with them at a local watering hole where boombas were the feature of Friday night gatherings. They hadn't gone to a session in several years and were sorry to find out that it was no longer an option as the place had closed.

Before we go any further, I need to tell you about boombas. A boomba is a musical instrument and is hand-crafted by dedicated artisans.

I couldn't find out much about them on the internet, except that they were originally called "devil's sticks." After getting acquainted with a boomba I've been unable to decide whether they were intended to summon the Devil or scare him away!

A boomba is, basically, a broomstick with appendages. The one I'm presently borrowing from Judith and Bill has, from the top down, a pair of cymbals with five jingle bells attached, placed horizontally at the top of the stick and held in place by a finial about six inches around with a beer company logo encircling it.

Under that is a gold-painted wooden block, about two by five inches, with a slot through the middle, followed by a tambourine with a hole on the side to hold a drumstick, followed by three large jingle bells near the bottom of the stick, just above the spring that allows the boomba to be bounced up and down. On the opposite side is a row of eleven large jingle bells attached to a leather strap which is attached to the stick.

This is a basic boomba, I understand. I've seen one with a bicycle horn attached, which is a very nice touch and lends a great deal to one's musical expression.

A friend tells me that his boomba (now gone to boomba heaven) had a little music rack near the top, an elegant touch when you think of how completely useless such an addition is.

The very best part of the boomba, to my way of thinking, is that one doesn't have to know squat about reading music to play it. All that's needed is a sense of rhythm and a lack of concern about making a fool of oneself in public.

He didn't know it at the time, but my friend Arturo was helping me cross boomba playing off my bucket list when he invited me to go to a meeting of a local boomba club at one of the senior residences nearby.

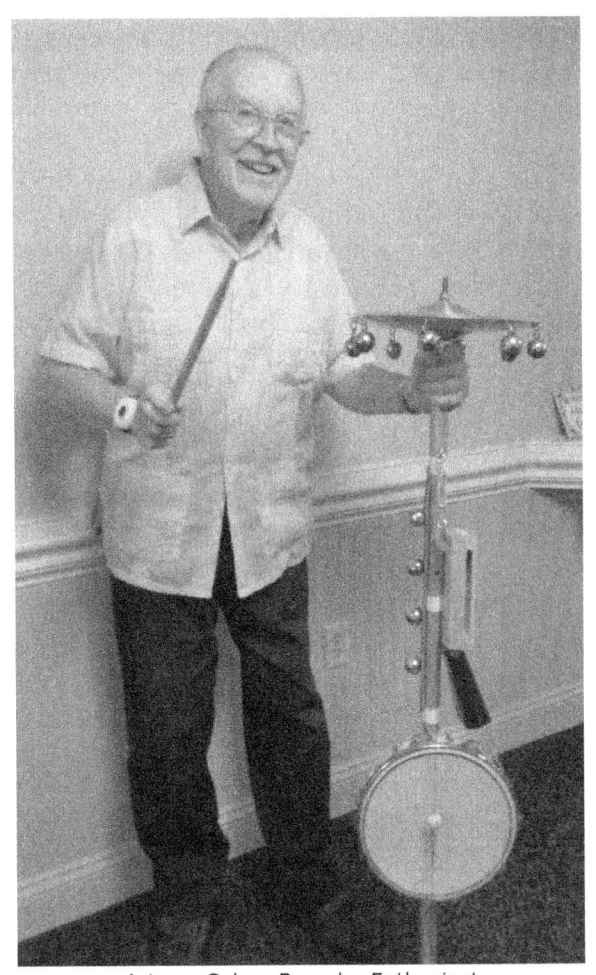

Arturo, Cuban Boomba Enthusiast

How much fun was that! We joined a group of ten experienced boomba players who did their thing to the tune of lively polka music, and I was enthralled.

I didn't even know I was harboring any frustration until I was able to slam it all out with my drumstick!

Is something troubling *you*, Bunky? Just find yourself a boomba and whack away at that thing until you don't remember what was on your mind when you began. There's absolutely nothing like slamming away on the tambourine, or the cymbals, or on the stick itself, to take all the energy out of any bad feelings you have.

A kind of fringe benefit was finding out that I am in better physical condition that I thought. After an hour of pumping that boomba up and down (this one had a piece of heavy rebar in place of the wooden broomstick) I expected to have a very sore arm the next day. But everything was in place and in working order the next morning and I even went to exercise class.

It saddens me to think that in the next generation or so the boomba may become extinct, along with the white rhino and some exotic birds of the Amazon. What a loss to humanity! Go and see if you can find a boomba to play before it's too late.

* * *

THE LURE OF WATER

A friend recently asked me why I enjoy our Lutherburgh swimming pool so much when I don't swim. Well, there are a few reasons, one of them being the availability of it, right here in the building. All I have to do is go downstairs to take advantage of it. Of course, finding someone to go with me, since the house rules require a buddy at all times, is another matter.

Another reason is that water exercises are so much easier than doing them on dry land. If I stand on one leg on the floor and fall down, it hurts! Not to mention that it's entirely possible to break something important if I go down. Also not to mention how difficult, if not impossible, it is to get up again! When I try that in the pool, the water eases the flop considerably; nothing fatal happens.

But the best reason is that it just feels so good! The temperature is just the way I like it, and sliding down into the water is a delightfully sensuous pleasure.

For lots of years my husband, the boys and I went to a beautiful lake in New Hampshire for a week or two every summer. The boys would wear themselves out and always fell asleep the minute they hit their beds. One evening my husband thought it would be a lot of fun to go skinny-dipping off the dock just down from the house. No one was at home in the house next door, and there was a lot of greenery separating us from the folks on the other side. We knew the kids wouldn't wake up, and this was a new adventure for me, so even though it seemed a little strange I decided, as I often do when something new is presented, "why not give it a try."

We waited until dark and walked down to the lake. My husband ran right off the end of the dock into the water. I wasn't going to do that; I had to take the steps at the side. I stood on the dock, took off my robe, and just enjoyed the feel of the cool air. This was beginning to seem like fun.

Suddenly I was enveloped in a blinding light! What was going on? Had I suddenly died and was heading into the light to meet my Maker in my birthday suit? Oh, if only!

Someone was out on the lake in a little cruiser with a very big light in front. Off the dock I went and tried to hide underneath it as the boat went by, mortified by the cheers of happy men. I never had the nerve to try skinny-dipping again, and it isn't on my bucket list, either.

New Hampshire Dock

Years back the women's magazines touted baths as the premier way to relax after a hard day's work. Light candles, they said, and place them around the tub. Throw in some bubble bath granules. Find some peaceful music to soothe the mind and soul. Pick up a book you haven't had time for, and just relax.

Well, that was fine and good if I ever had time to stay there! With kids needing someone to help them find their homework, and the ironing waiting, peace was hard to come by and I gave up the idea after a few tries.

When I was single again, it wasn't sensible to indulge in expensive, mood-setting bathroom candles and bath salts. On the other hand, being alone in the house meant that I could leave the bathroom door open in order to hear the phone, just in case a better offer came my way. Being out with friends was better than a solitary evening in a rapidly-cooling bathtub any time.

Now that I'm old and living at Lutherburgh, things have changed once again. I can't take a bath here even if I want to, since I don't have a bathtub anymore. This is not a complaint. I love my walk-in shower.

Some apartments (not mine) have a second bathroom with a tub, and that inspires thoughts once more of candlelit bathing, but I *know,* without a doubt, that if I got myself seated in a bathtub these days I would never be able to get back out.

How embarrassing would it be to have to pull the "call chain" and wait for someone from the maintenance department to haul me out! Would I be able to reach a towel before anyone showed up? What if it were so late at night that the maintenance department was closed? Would the night guard come up? I'd never be able to face him again. If all else failed, would someone call 911? How insane would that be!

So for me, anyway, the bathtub is a thing of the past (one among many, sorry to say). Now if you are a little person who can haul yourself around with impunity maybe this whole story makes no sense to you at all.

It's probably worth mentioning that someone I know keeps her stash of booze in her spare bathroom. If the collection gets too big, the overflow is consigned to the bathtub. She doesn't want all that unused space to go to waste.

Booze in the Bathroom

Emergency Stash

All I can say about that is "good for you," and I mean it sincerely.

* * *

THE SHOW MUST GO ON

Since moving to Lutherburgh I've had the opportunity to perform at several concerts put on by our community Chorus. Perform is a generous word for what I've been doing. I tend to think of it more as acting ridiculous in order to amuse the residents.

I've been a cowgirl flirting with the members of a men's quartet, and a harried shopper, trying to get it all done before Christmas. More recently I've been a "Sweet Violet," accompanying the song with a playlet of sorts, acting silly with friends Bob and Dave. It was definitely less intimidating with two other people being silly, too. The way to do this is, I've discovered, don't make eye contact with anyone in the room. If you're being ridiculous anyway, it helps to cross your eyes.

The Farmer, the Father and Sweet Violet

My favorite role at Lutherburgh was the one I played last holiday season. I was a Christmas tree, prancing around to the tune of "O Tannenbaum" but with a different set of words. It was a great chance to try out my ballet moves, even though the handmade costume was sort of heavy.

Oh! Christmas Tree?

It seems that being a ham comes naturally to me. When I was a little kid and my parents and I lived in the Republican Club headquarters in Bensonhurst, Brooklyn, my bedroom had a closet set back under a dormer, and when my cousins came to visit we would jam ourselves in there and decide what kind of a play we wanted to present.

We then assembled the parents and insisted that they endure our performances, which would all begin by our exiting the closet in a line, oldest to youngest.

I have no recollection of what our little plays were about, or my role in any of them, but knowing my cousins, who were all older than me, I suspect I was usually the fool of choice.

The nascent performer in me remained dormant for several years, until as a fourth grader I desperately wanted to play the part of the Infanta of Spain in our class production. I lost the role to a prettier and slimmer girl and though I don't recall any of the dialog which I so painstakingly memorized, I do remember the name of the female who stole my stardom from me.

About that time I joined the Girl Scouts, and our fearless leader decided we should present a minstrel show. This wasn't an inappropriate activity back in the 1940s, and I was lucky to escape the messy blackface makeup when I became Mr. Interlocutor. Our performance was a roaring success, and the audience enjoyed it so much that we had two more of them later. Each time I was the interlocutor, and from then on I was hooked.

Teen years presented more opportunities for showing off in our JIFFLE group, and I took full advantage of it. Then I settled down as a happy housewife and mother and forgot about The Stage for a few years. Then one evening, just wanting to get out of the house for a few hours, I left my husband in charge of the kiddies and attended a women's group meeting at church. I was still a member of that group when I left Long Island for Lutherburgh, but we stopped performing several years prior so I was out of practice when I arrived here.

There were more than 100 women in the group in the early 50s, and we had some really fun times together. For several years we had wonderful mother-daughter parties every Mothers' Day. The one I remember best was when we decided to make Mary Poppins our theme.

The movie had recently come out, and we planned our mother-daughter party to include a fantastic home baked cake made by one of the members, with cut-out and hand-decorated cookies of the characters on top, balloons and umbrellas hanging from the ceiling of the Fellowship Hall, and silver plated teaspoons with Mary Poppins on the handle that came free of charge from some company doing a special promotion.

Mary Poppins

As a mother of sons, who would have otherwise been excluded from the party, I was drafted to be Mary Poppins herself, complete with parrot head umbrella made by the extraordinary cake baker, one of my old Easter hats, white blouse and blue skirt with crinoline (saved for eons from teenage days), and high top boots. Years later one of the now-grown-up little girls told me that she and her sisters thought I really was Mary Poppins.

I got through the whole performance by speaking the words of "Supercalifragilisticexpialidocious" rather than attempting to sing them, but, as I have been known to do, got too full of myself and tried to say it backwards. From there the whole thing went south for me, but the little girls didn't seem to notice.

Over the years, in varying productions put on by our women's group, I was Fred Astaire once, also a silent screen idol, and Ginger Rogers on another occasion, Mary Poppins again with a bottle of scotch rather than a spoonful of sugar, a bewildered woman at an abstract art show, Hansel for a take-off on *Into the Woods*, a wooly lamb (as in the *Whiffenpoof Song*), a member of a backwoods jug band, Lucy in my favorite episode, her TV commercial for *Vitameatavegemin*, and several other roles that have left my mind, at least for the time being.

Silent Movie Star Cleans Up After the Show

When I first moved to Lutherburgh I thought I would have to act staid and quiet and mature in order to fit in, but as it turns out there are a lot of easygoing folks around here who enjoy a bit of silliness as much as I do. That was really good to know, because I've been having lots of fun here ever since.

Whiffenpoofs in Action, author far right

If you're not having fun, get out there and find yourself a party. Revisit your bucket list and see what you can cross off next!

* * *

WORST WINTER EVER!

I think …. I may …. go MAD! This is me, with wild gesticulations, greeting the morning at five twenty-five a.m. with that *sound* chilling my soul. Right under my bedroom window! Scrape, scrape, scrape, beep, beep, beep. More scraping, more beeping. Now there's scraping and beeping at the same time! When is it going to stop? When will this torture end? You fellow residents know what I'm talking about. It snowed again last night.

There's no point in trying to go back to sleep. I think this sound may haunt my dreams well into the summer. It occurs to me that I may be caught up somehow in the movie "Groundhog Day," where Bill Murray wakes up at the same time each morning to the mellow tones of Sonny Bono singing *I've Got You, Babe*, and relives Groundhog Day over and over again until he gets it right.

There's no chance of sleeping so I get up, make some tea, and sit on my sofa looking out the balcony doors. There are two bright, shiny eyes coming at me. Since it's still dark I can't make it out too well, but it looks like the squat little snow mover. Oops. There it goes again, beep, beep, beep. Yes, it's backing up. The lights on the front are high up in the air. The lights on the back are closer to the ground and have two little red ones on either side of them.

I wonder briefly why I'm paying so much attention to this. Is it some perverse desire to know the form of my tormentor? Am I beginning to experience Stockholm Syndrome, where I am learning to love the thing that feels like it's killing me?

Snow Removal

Please understand, I'm not complaining, just sharing some thoughts. The only time I complained was during the first of the many snow storms we had, when the cleanup crews were out blowing the snow off our cars with leaf blowers at 2 a.m. It never happened again at that ungodly hour. And I have to remember that my car will be clear of snow and ice when, and if, I decide to go out! So I know that we are being well cared for, and I'll just have to find a way to deal with the scrapes and beeps until this never-ending winter is over. Hoping you are doing the same.

* * *

CHRISTMAS MEMORIES

Christmas in Brooklyn in 1941 was magical. Wartime or not, as a six-year-old I had no idea that all was not right with the world.

Fifth Avenue in Bay Ridge was impossibly fine, with one brightly decorated holiday shop after another. When the snow drifted down, and the sky turned the darkest blue that ever was, enchantment glittered and beckoned from every store window. I remember a moon, but possibly there was none. But there must have been a moon, otherwise how could everything have been so purely beautiful?

What would be the most wonderful thing in the whole wide world to give to Mama on Christmas Eve? My father and I stopped and pondered silently at each store window. We compared the merits of every pretty bracelet in the jewelry store. We peeked inside the lingerie shop, where they had those exquisitely soft nightgowns with the long sleeves and the bows at the neck. With such a plethora of riches, how could we possibly choose? Eventually the nightgown was placed gently in the beautiful, pure white box with bunches of tissue paper cradling its pretty pastel lushness. I took the package from the saleswoman's hands with the reverence such a wonderful gift deserved.

Daddy was a comforting presence. I could put my mittened hand in his pocket and know that nothing bad would ever touch me. The very large man with row upon row of Christmas trees hovering around him held no danger for me. I boldly chose the tree

I liked the best, mustering up the courage to ask the price and pass that information along to my father. Miracle of miracles, the price was exactly the amount he had intended to spend.

With the snow turning to slush under our feet, we glided along the pavement, heading for the pretty lady on the corner with the red cape and the big, jangling bell. At her side, the young man with the trumpet puffed up his cheeks preparing to inspire the passersby to drop their coins into the enormous red cauldron. Oh, the excitement of that golden horn! And how satisfying the clink of the nickels that I was allowed to toss into the kettle.

Daddy hoisted the tree onto his shoulder, while I skipped along by his side, clutching the bag with Mama's gift inside. No night has ever been quite so perfect in exactly that way since.

*** * *

Acknowledgments

My thanks go out to the members of the writers group at Luther Crest retirement community in Allentown, Pennsylvania, which at this writing consists of Marianne and Manfred Bahmann, Paul Buehrle, Judith Ruhe Diehl, David Godshall, Marion Kayhart, Bob Kearney, Mary Jane Martin, Nancy McCain and Don Moore. Without their urging and encouragement I would never have started this book.

Special thanks to Marianne Bahmann who walked me through the process step by step and made it possible for me to both start and complete the job. Truly, it wouldn't have happened without her! Thanks also to Judith Ruhe Diehl who was a willing and most proficient editor and proofreader, friend, and inspiration.

Thanks to the family of the late George R. Dickson for permission to use an example of George's wonderfully creative mind as the title page art for this book.

Thanks also to friends and family who weren't sure what I was doing but were encouraging nonetheless.

And thanks be to God that I lived long enough to get it done!

About the Author

Helen Wernlund was born and raised in Brooklyn, New York, an only child of Swedish emigrant parents. In an effort to amuse herself lacking siblings to torment she wrote stories and read them to her elementary school peers where they were generally well received. In high school she wrote a regular column for the school newspaper and was co-editor of her senior yearbook. Several years later, married and the mother of two little boys, she wrote a weekly column for a local newspaper on Long Island, where the family then lived. As a "cradle Lutheran" Helen became very involved with her congregation and started a church library, choosing the books and writing publicity for the church newsletter.

Inspired by the feminist movement in the late 1960s Helen developed an interest in advocacy for women and directed her newly-awakened desire to get educated in that direction.

After a divorce in 1984, Helen completed work on a Bachelor's degree in Community and Human Services from Empire State College where she became serious about writing papers for her classes. A few years later, after what seemed like a lifetime of writing papers, she received a Master's degree in Social Work from the State University of New York at Stony Brook. In the meantime she met her life partner and they were together until his death in 2008.

Her M.S.W. degree led to her most productive and satisfying working years: at a displaced homemaker center and later in domestic violence agencies doing individual and group counseling, education and outreach.

In 2001 after a two-year course of study and writing another raft of papers she became a Synodical Deacon in the Metropolitan New York Synod of the Evangelical Lutheran Church in America, doing ministry for victims of domestic violence and raising awareness as chair of the Synodical Task Force.

After relocating to Allentown, Pennsylvania Helen became actively engaged in the life of Luther Crest Continuing Care Retirement Community where she writes for the newsletter and literary publication. These days she also enjoys writing *Letters to the Editor* and composing submissions to the paper's *Best Bad Writers in the Lehigh Valley* contest as well as participating in domestic violence awareness ministry at her Lutheran church in Allentown.

Helen has no idea where life will take her next, but she looks forward to the journey.

* * *